TRADITION, CULTURE &
UNDERDEVELOPMENT OF AFRICA

by

Udobata R Onunwa

Published 2005 by arima publishing

www.arimapublishing.com

ISBN 1-84549-056-8

Printed and bound in the United Kingdom

Typeset in Garamond 10/14

arima publishing
ASK House, Northgate Avenue
Bury St Edmunds, Suffolk IP32 6BB
t: (+44) 01284 700321

www.arimapublishing.com

DEDICATION

To all who loved and still love Africa
And have laboured to see her develop.

TABLE OF CONTENTS

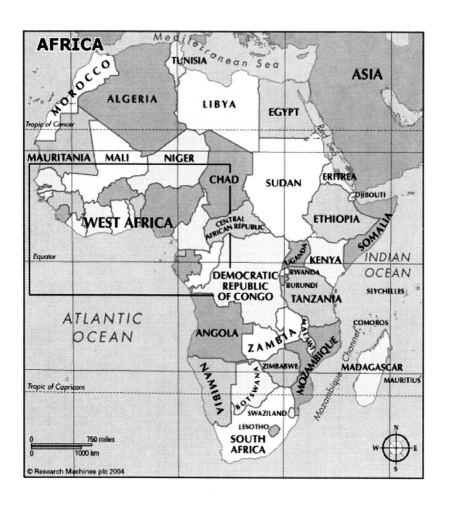

Map of Africa

PREFACE

The primary research that gave birth to this book was neither out for a polemic against a people's culture or religion nor an apologetic defence for them. It is rather a constructive evaluation of some basic principles and practices that need to be changed. This work aims at stimulating patriotic African leaders, men and women of goodwill and friends of Africa who desire and long for new ways to improve the current trends of degeneration in living standard of the people. There is a long history of *nationalist struggles* and *attempts* by Africans to defend and protect many of their cherished traditions from the onslaught of external agents of change. Often, most of the nationalist and indigenous approaches to the search for ways to defend and improve what is authentically African had taken militant and aggressive approach. Some of them yielded positive results but not all. A new nationalist stance needs to be taken now in the face of prevailing circumstances and especially as we begin the first few years of the 21st century. We have observed that any indigenous scholar or patriot who does not take the popular *militant posture* of his colleagues or come out to *glorify his people's past* is looked upon by others as either, *brainwashed or Euro-centric*. It is important to remark that one should know where to draw the line between blind nationalism and objective self-examination or reflection on one's strategies, thoughts and methods. It is not right to praise either systems or people in power always when we know that there is need for some creative and constructive changes that can improve the system.

Many Africans enjoy hearing beautiful stories of how Africa was *developing, growing, progressing* on her own path before she was impacted upon by European conquests, colonization and missionary invasion. African society was stable and peaceful until the disruptive power of the European merchants; colonial administrators and missionaries brought disaster to her. That is not the picture Chinua Achebe, the renowned Nigerian novelist was trying to portray in his popular novel, **Things Fall Apart.** Static and probably an *unchanging* African society was a myth. Africans and their foreign friends who are truly seeking ways to entrench lasting democratic system and stability, social and economic progress and development in Africa and for Africans must as a matter of fact begin to look for some new ways and methods to achieve this noble and laudable goal. A critical review of the factors that kept Africa back from *moving up the social ladder along* with other parts of the world is now long overdue. This evaluation calls for a sincere spirit of self-examination (not self-condemnation), which is important for any positive step forward.

The present writer has gleaned from various sources to project his own viewpoint. The sources include materials from history, philosophy, sociology, anthropology, economics, political science and religion. An objective critical analysis of data from these sources has been made and from it a new viewpoint is projected. It is believed that those who are genuinely planning to build clean society in Africa might find the views herein expressed helpful. If on the other hand, this work generates a sort of controversy that can bring long term positive challenge to policy makers, scholars and true patriotic citizens, it has achieved one of its aims. Some controversies generate self-awareness, and self-awareness generates self- improvement. There is therefore an urgent need for Africans to rethink why and how certain things are going the way they are now.

European conquest of Africa brought in many negative effects and influences. It destroyed the people's cherished traditions and culture and diverted Africa from her own-charted path of *progress* and *development*. The present study does not intend to gloss over those negative aspects of European presence in Africa. Yet it is important to note that an aspect of that presence brought in many other benefits. The positive effects are overwhelming. *Acculturation* has immensely affected Africa in many ways. By *acculturation*, we mean the transformation of a culture through the introduction of new elements, whether they are physical tools, techniques, new religious ideas, or new systems of authority and control. *Acculturation* involves an amalgam between the old elements and a new introduction. It may, in other words, imply a process of changing *tribal, simple and unsophisticated* lifestyle through the impact of outside conquering culture and civilisation. The method of conquest could be in the form of military force or peaceful and gradual process of infiltration. Predominantly, it is a change that takes place in rural communities. A new set of values comes to compete with the old and they present a people with a new choice because of contact with external change-agents.

The penetration of Africa by Europeans came with great technological revolution and the emergence of a world community that, unlike the internal movements, (which included inter-tribal wars, primary and secondary migrations, etc.) brought Africa into the mainstream of *developments*. European presence and influence had played enormous role in altering African societies through secondary effects of technological innovation.

In the *undislocated* African societies, the religion of the ancestors determined the world-views, life style and thought-pattern. On the other hand, western societies had for long been shaped and transformed by the transcendental and revolutionary power and influence of Christianity. African societies can be described as *primal, conservative* and *underdeveloped*. Africa was one of the *Cradles of Civilization* of the Ancient World, and by that very fact, the birthplace of humanity. Her achievements in prehistoric times were enormous. Yet, she could not go far enough in her struggles to survive the onslaught of many internal and external agents of change.

A new Africa is emerging from the old. The colonial era has ended but neo-imperialism is still operating in many ways. The new independent states of Africa inherited the geographical boundaries created by the Colonial Powers that partitioned the continent between them and ruled them as they (the Powers) wanted. What we call *countries* in Africa are collections of various types of people lumped together for the administrative convenience of the **conquerors**. So they have patterned the new institutions of government after those of the various European countries that ruled them, although the methods in which they operate vary in many ways from the ones they inherited from their former rulers. The Spirit of nationalism and accountability is yet to be established in many of those countries. Avery negligible percentage of new nation -states in Africa abandoned the system of government they inherited from the colonial administrators and opted for some radical systems that did not last. The reasons are both external and internal and are beyond the scope of this survey.

There is an extensive economic expansion and one also notices incipient industrialisation in many places although civil wars and political instability have destroyed lives and property. The new sovereign states in Africa are making friends with many other nations of the world according to their needs and other opportunities, without risking the friendship and love of their former colonial rulers. Africa is *coming of age*, forming continental and regional economic and political organisations. Yet she does not compare in any way with the West in food production, health care delivery, communications, literacy, industrialisation, life expectancy, transport and income per capita.

The West has considerably changed her former pejorative description of Africa as the *Dark Continent* to either Third *World,* or *Developing Nation.* These new names may be a polite way to express hidden spite and insult or a *refined way of trying to avoid causing offence* by trying to be *nice.* It may be a genuine way to accept Africa as a partner in international affairs and programmes. Definitely, the whole implication boils down to the fact that Africa, which used to host one of the *Cradles of Civilisation,* lost her ancient glory and power at a point in time and fell into a state of u*nderdevelopment.*

Africa had her mode of writing, for instance, the **Hieroglyphics,** which flourished around the Nile Valley and the **Nsibidi** around the South Eastern Nigeria sub-culture area, among others. Yet these are no longer in use. Traces of good and effective legal system, agriculture, communication, dance, culture, healing practices, which were traditional to Africa have been found in many places where people depended on them as functional ways of lifestyle. Those who have supported the projection of African past attribute the loss of the rich mine of culture and civilisation and the present state of *underdevelopment* to European conquest and colonisation. That is not the only cause of the decline of the erstwhile popular African empires. The current problem of *underdevelopment* is interplay of several factors that were largely controlled by the religious systems that nurtured and directed life in Africa. It is this *traditional religion and culture* that is supremely responsible for the present problem of *underdevelopment.* A *monocausal* explanation or interpretation is not usually comprehensive, but for Africa whose traditional religious system is all- embracing, her religious traditions and culture, more than any other factor, brought her to the present state of poverty and underdevelopment.

We all know that Africa is, until now poor, her economy is stunted, her social patterns are largely primitive and her people are mostly illiterate. These are basic conditions of her past and present. This study will among other things, check the repetition of the same cycle in future. The tragic cycle of poverty repeats itself ceaselessly- malnutrition, ill-health, disease, lack of sanitary and medical facilities, inadequate skills and techniques, lack of capital and an economy that is based on low-standard subsistence production or an export industry from which Africans derive a low meagre living wage.[1] We should not see the above assessment and impression as an exaggeration but a picture of what is prevailing in many places. More than fifty years ago, the United Nations conducted a survey, which revealed that:

> *Africa as a whole is economically among the least developed areas of the world, with low levels of production and consumption.*[2]

The situation has worsened in recent years with military dictatorships, abuse of Human Rights, heavy debt burden and unbridled corruption of those in high positions, ecological disaster, civil wars and the scourge of HIV/ AIDS. As already stated, many people still lay huge blames on European conquests and colonisation and continuous interference into African affairs, as the chief if not the only factor responsible for the present state of economic stagnation and general *underdevelopment.* This is to us now an over flogged excuse which many Africans easily proffer to free themselves from any form of responsibility to the continuous state of degeneration of standard of living in the continent. Consequently, there has been a loud cry for **Reparations** of the looted wealth from Africa during the period of Slave Trade and colonial administration. Many who champion this view find it difficult to believe that other internal factors might have been involved too. Ridiculously, we have observed that sometimes, those who blame foreign Powers for the misfortune of Africa had at one time or the other, contributed heavily to the misfortune of their home people. Many did this through illegal massive export of the local currency to other countries of the world or by using their public offices to amass large wealth at the detriment of the poor. Some colluded with foreign business partners to rip off enormous wealth from their countries. Many have never analysed the dysfunctional roles of the traditional religion and culture.

The traditional religion and culture is the bedrock of African cosmology. African scholars, who out of sheer nationalism still exalt all aspects of this traditional religion and culture, have not critically and objectively looked at its negative roles in historical perspective. It is the traditional religion and culture, which not only formed the basis of African philosophy and conceptual schemes, but also largely *controlled, determined,* and *directed* the thought-pattern and ways of life.

We are taking a different view from the usual popular one held by most people. We are, therefore, offering an explanation and propounding the thesis that *the inherent nature and characteristics of African traditional religion and culture, which could not face the challenges of another powerful and conquering culture, was the chief agent responsible for Africa's constant underdevelopment in modern world.* Those who still look for reasons or factors responsible for the underdevelopment of Africa outside the traditional religion and culture do not seem to understand the powerful influence of the religion in African society. It is time for Africans to look inwards and re-examine their ways and thought pattern to assess the reasons for the persistent stagnant growth and progress in society. If Africa would change from being Consumer-oriented Third – World nation to that of Industrialised and Developed Continent, she would no longer allow her traditional religion and culture to *determine, direct and control* her thoughts and conceptual scheme. Many developed nations of the world are no longer operating with their traditional and primary religious ideas. Africa and Africans can initiate new ideas, projects and programmes, but the problem is that of sustainability. That is why many inventions and cultural civilisations experienced a short-life span before they were forced into extinction or collapse completely. This is pathetic particularly when one thinks of many erstwhile big empires and inventions that have disappeared. This view may sound judgmental and dogmatic but we have sustained it with strong data from the field. One notices a lot of ruined architectural sites, abandoned industrial villages and buried artefacts in many obscure villages in Africa. Some of them were destroyed by wars or ecological disasters but it is important to ask why such big projects could not last. As already stated, many developed and industrialised nations are no longer operating with their conservative traditional primary world-views. Those nations had contacts with Christianity at a point in time. Such contacts transformed as well as reshaped their worldviews. Invariably, that led to a form of Renaissance and the dawn of a new era that had been going from strength to strength. For instance, a close look at some of the legal systems of some western countries shows evidence of Christian ethos and morals as the basic foundations of societal growth. This is a fact of history that many people in such countries seem to ignore or take for granted. Although the traditional religion and culture initiated and preserved some elements that made commendable contributions to the development of precolonial Africa, we must not forget its dysfunctional roles that also proved a hindrance to growth and further progress.

There is an uneven distribution of development projects in some parts of Africa, particularly in the West African sub-region. Westernisation and development are not synonymous but western education and civilisation formed part of the Christian package, which was bequeathed to the African converts. Regions and communities, which either fully or partially accepted the Christian faith and its ethos and vibrant and dynamic worldview rose high in modern western education and seemed to occupy key positions in commerce and industry. Those who preferred other systems did not go so far. This may be one of the reasons why there is complaint *of marginalisation* by some peoples in many countries. This does not in any why imply that other forms of civilisation or education did not or does not lead to human progress and development. The point we are stressing is that Western education, nurtured and sustained by the transforming power of Christianity in human history, has for a long time been used as a standard and objective measuring in international business transactions, politics and economy. The objective index of measuring development and progress in Africa is no longer the traditional pattern set by the ancestors several centuries back before contacts with the West and Christianity. We must state here that Christianity is not synonymous with the West. Both are different but are interrelated. Christianity influenced the West and transformed it, to some extent, into what it is today. In the same way, the West has given Christianity a Western face, a feature that has both positive and negative effects. On the positive side, Christianity permeates every culture, transforms it and incarnates itself in it. Thus, it becomes relevant and contextual to every culture. On the negative side, a particular culture that had hosted and domesticated Christian virtues and ethos should not look down on other cultures or impose its own values on others as if they are Christian per se. That is the problem of Western Christianity in many non-Western countries. But the hope is that since Christianity influenced the West for good and transformed it into modern developed nation states, it can do similar things in Africa and transform its systems of life and thought.

Africa is a large continent and obviously the second largest in the world. Its large and variant terrain is the home of many millions of people, a variety of cultures and languages. It is estimated that about 20% of the world's population live in Africa, although AIDS had depleted this in the recent past. In the North are the ruins and relics of Classic Civilisation; in the South is a history of more than four hundred years of European occupation and of struggle for liberation and independence (which has of late yielded valuable results). Between, lies the area that gave Africa the sobriquet of *Dark Continent*, a term that is no longer used in many serious academic and political discussions. The impact of culture and institutions of the colonial administration had been very great on the western-trained and educated elite who are now the heirs of the colonial power in Africa. Although Africans are steadily rising in the *developmental hierarchy*, the essential African contributions to the present World Order in technology, scientific discoveries, invention and industrial growth, besides resources of the earth itself, had been bare labour force. It is, therefore, obvious that in the present circumstances, *Africa is underdeveloped.* That is a known fact but the question is: *why is she like that or why has she remained like that?* The answer one gives depends on a number of factors particularly one's orientation. The nagging question that many Africans of several generations have been asking is: *Where Africa?* Although the question is not new, in our contemporary period, we might add, *where Africa in the scheme of human, social, technological and industrial development?* Every generation of Africans had been looking for answers to this question in their own way. The world is gradually being turned into a *global village*, the distance between one part of the world and the other, is gradually being reduced. This is the age of computer, yet many people in Africa are still picking nuts and fruits in the jungle while their leaders are busy importing war implements from Europe, America and the Far East for ceaseless and aimless fratricidal wars. At the same time, some of the leaders are opening huge personal bank accounts in many European capitals.

The loss of Africa's wealth and glory is not factually a one-off event but an on-going process. It is also connected with her inability to manage and protect her assets.

This management crisis is invariably linked to their limited ability to project far into the distant future-a very serious defect embedded in her cosmology.

Many Africans, including black nationalists, culture historians and archaeologists would reject this notion of a pre-colonial Africa. They could give endless litany of the achievements of Africa. Certainly some could be easily mentioned. Her darkness and under-development were a historical event not a *natural phenomenon.* It is evident, however, that in the hands of many European historians, the history of Africa is primarily concentrated on the conquest of the continent. They had thus left to the anthropologist any discussions on events purely African. Therefore, many European scholars have used the teaching and study of history in this sense as a means to justify European cultural superiority. African nationalists, have reacted in a different way by extolling their ancestors who resisted European invasion as heroic and have created a past which gains intellectual justification for modern national aspiration. They, thus, try to *justify and glorify the African past* in its totality. Both the European scholars who exaggerated the negative aspects of the African society and the Africans, who reacted in the way we have just stated, did not present a balanced view of the situation. Thomas Hodgkin aptly summarised the ennoblement of the African past in his *Nationalism in Colonial Africa*.

He expressed the views of most African Nationalists when he stated that:

> *Perhaps, the most important and deeply-felt aspect of the nationalist answer to the myth of African barbarism is the stress placed on the qualities of the pre-European African societies; their achievement in such fields as the plastic arts work in gold, bronze and ivory music and dancing, folk story and poetry; the complexity and depth of their religious beliefs and metaphysics, the conception of the community as consisting of the dead, the living and the unborn; their rational attitude to sexual relations and to the place of women in society, their delight in children and reverence to the aged, their view of education as a process of continuing through life; their dislike of autocracy and their delicate political mechanisms for securing the expansion and adjustment of different interests and wills.*[3]

It is evident that the potentials and valuable qualities of the African life and the achievements of some of the ancestors were enormous. But the problem is the inability of the African social system to develop into a culture that could have been seen and copied as standard by other nations of the world, a technology that could have been transferred to other countries, an economy that could have been the reference term for international trade and commerce. It is, likely perhaps, that if Europeans did not invade Africa, the pre-European form of progress and civilisation could have continued in the continent without necessarily being imposed on any outside world nor degenerated and declined as it did. On the other hand, if European presence did not change the African way of life *by military conquest*, necessity and circumstance could have led the Africans to be more adventurous and creative in their own way. Probably these could have maintained a form of development that could have been slow but directional and stable. These are mere speculations.

The main materials for this work were collected through field research, library sources and oral interviews. During the period, I spent part of my research leave at the School of Oriental and African Studies (S.O.A.S), London. I had the opportunity to discuss extensively with a number of scholars; some of them have now retired. For instance, Professor J. Richard Gray, of History Department, Mr. Winston of Africa Department and Professor E. G. Parrinder, were helpful at different points in time. It was a privilege for me to meet with them at various stages of the work. I spent part of my Sabbatical leave in Tanzania at the Lutheran Theological University College, Mukumira and used the period to visit many East and South African communities to collect data to update the work. I spent a good time in the University of Birmingham archives and the Selly Oak Colleges Orchard and Learning and Research Centre when I was the Director for the Centre for Christian Education and Church Management at Westhill College of the University of Birmingham.

During the extensive research trips, I had immense opportunities to consult scholars at conferences, workshops and seminars. Many of them offered useful suggestions and criticisms. I am also thankful to my undergraduate and postgraduate students at the University of Nigeria Nsukka, University of Calabar Nigeria, and Lutheran University Theological College, Makumira, Tanzania and School of Mission and World Christianity, Selly Oak Colleges, Birmingham UK and Trinity College, University of Bristol, UK. Some of them through field trips, tutorials and seminars helped me with useful data. Some of them had earlier read part of this work in drafts and strongly made their views known. Their disagreements and criticisms on several occasions made me redefine my stand on certain issues. Selly Oak offered me opportunity for multi-cultural contacts. There is no greater reward or stimulus to a teacher than the response of awakened minds. I also owe a lot of thanks to Professors Ogbu U.Kalu, late Emefie Ikenga-Metuh, Edmund Ilogu, R. Slenczka and Frank I. Benz for their help at different stages of the work.

I am grateful to Pacific Publishers, Obosi-Nigeria, and Thesen Verlag Wowincle Darmstadt Germany for publishing my other works without asking me to pay anything. My wife Dorothy has been sponsoring most of my trips overseas for research and collection of data. The Theological Education Fund, of the World Council of Churches offered some little financial aid during my stay in London. The Warden of Medical Missionary Association Hostel in Islington London was very kind on two occasions I lived there during the field trips for this work. I am grateful to Mrs. Victoria Ifeanyi-Eze for spending time to type and retype the draft after each correction.

Udobata Onunwa
Selly Oak Colleges
University of Birmingham, UK

NOTES

1. Rupert Emerson   The character of American Interest in Africa in W.Goldochruchst (ed.) *The United States and Africa.* (London & New York: F. Praeger) 1962, p. ii
2. Rupert Emerson   ibid; p. 11 – 12
3. Rupert Emerson   op.cit. 219- 220

SECTION ONE

CHAPTER ONE
Functional Definition of Terms

1.1 Concepts of Development and Underdevelopment

The key concept of this book is *Development* from which we derive such other terms as *Under-development, Developing,* etc. Africa is at present described as a *developing continent,* which in other words, implies that she is in the process of developing or rising to reach the level already attained by countries in the West. The term *development* is comparatively new in Social Sciences. Its technical and functional meaning acquired new dimension and significance since the end of the Second World War.[1] There seems to be an almost complete absence of the term in the field of Social Sciences. Many scholars, especially social-anthropologists and ethnographers cautiously avoided giving a definition because they did not want to make it an appellation in contra-distinction to *Dark Continent* and *Under-developed* which were used previously in a pejorative sense. Missionary writings also politely avoided it. As used currently in the Social Sciences, *development* is a total social process, which includes economic, political, cultural and social growth.[2]

The term *development,* with time, has synthesised the aspirations of people for improved human living conditions. Thus it has become synonymous with increased wealth or at best a higher level of well-being. It is in this perspective that Myrdal defined it to mean the *movement upwards of the entire social system.*[3] This presupposes a dialectical process and stage in the movement - a process by which all factors involved and like in the case of tradition and culture, imply a functional unity by which advances in one area mean advances in others, and conversely, the stagnation of one retards the growth of the rest. For instance, injustices in a social system might breed social disharmony. A disruption of social justice and fair play can disrupt peaceful and conducive atmosphere for increased production and achievement. On individual level, Walter Rodney states that development implies increased *skill and capacity, greater freedom, creativity, self-discipline, responsibility and material well being.*[4]

Development, which is a complex and multi-dimensional phenomenon, embraces more than mere institutional progress. Some people have for long used institutional progress as the empirical and objective standard of measuring growth, well being and success. It involves elevation of the entire social system. This implies that development incorporates a feature in which an entire community is involved including the ways they do *their things and the environment* in which they operate. In other words, development is both *man- oriented and institution-oriented.*[5]

It means on one hand, that such elevation in the social system is for the well being of man and the improvement of his environs. In many cases, development has been understood to be synonymous with industrialisation, *urbanisation* and *modernisation* as we see them today in many countries. These are quite good if they serve the physical, moral and intellectual as well as spiritual well-being of humans in society, but would mean nothing if they create a situation where humanity is crushed in the wheel of individual or group manipulation and tyranny. Technological progress means nothing if it is turned into an industry for production of implements that would lead to mass destruction of life and property in a world where hunger and disease threaten a sizeable percentage of human population. But if it is used to produce implements that can improve life expectancy, food, shelter and health care, then technology is a mark of human and social development. Thus development understood in this sense should not be turned into an instrument of destruction of the world and human life in it.

An upward movement of entire ecological and human factors could be better described as *social development.* Two aspects of it are noticeable. One is socio-cultural and the other human. Both may not necessarily depend so much on the level of industrialisation. Hence, habits could be cultivated and the value of man as *sacred being* meticulously respected and upheld. A society in which the rights and dignity of individual persons are religiously respected could be said to be developed. If the societal tools and crafts are somewhat sophisticated, it could be described as a *developed society* with a relatively high standard of living.

From a nationalist's point of view, therefore, Africa was *culturally developed* before her rich natural and human resources were destroyed by European powers that shared the countries and ruled them as if they were their personal property. To many Africans, that was the beginning of their people's misfortune. Prior to that, the Slave Trade which ravaged Africa for over three hundred years left her in shambles.

The term *underdevelopment* is not necessarily the opposite of *development*. It is also different from such derogatory terms like *backward, primitive* or *native*, used by some earlier writers for people other than themselves. It is discovered that among many economic theorists, *under-development* does not mean the same as underdeveloped *or undeveloped*. The term underdevelopment is rather seen from a historical viewpoint as a state in which an exploited or oppressed and defeated society is left by those superior powers that ruled her. It is a condition that grew out of the relations between two people on unequal terms, for instance the relations between colonial powers and their colonies.[6] Norman Ashcraft had argued that *underdeveloped* refers to a state of relative poverty within a given society while *underdevelopment* implies a set of political and economic conditions making for such poverty.[7] It is, therefore, a bye-product of history of relationship between one country and the other. The nationalist historians and economists who attribute the *underdevelopment* of Africa to the *monocausal* factor of European presence in Africa often neglect some internal factors that prevailed before the arrival of external change agents. Some of the internal factors were inter-tribal or ethnic wars, human sacrifice, etc. which set in a process of gradual decay before the final onslaught by foreign powers totally destroyed the traditional and important land-marks. Some other important internal factors were the social and cultural institutions, practices, and values that were created by the traditional religious system that underpinned the African cosmology. Those who accuse European political interests as the chief factor of *underdevelopment* of Africa also condemn the Christian Missionaries as agents of colonisation. African nationalist writers have always insisted that each mission station was an exercise in colonisation.[8] The intra and inter-ethnic skirmishes and wars also contributed to the evils of European Slave Trade. Some local agents and chiefs helped the slave dealers to capture fellow Africans who were carried away into the New World as slaves.

Although Western Europe had for long acquired the energy to transform the world from the spirit of Christianity which strives to incorporate itself in humanity and renew the face of the earth, one cannot include colonisation, the spread of Western capitalism and the imposition of Western Languages and cultures in the movement of Christian world renewal.[9] Where such a thing happened, it could be a mere co-incidence or accident of history, an exception rather than the rule. This is not to say that some Christian missionaries were completely apolitical or were not at times involved in some complexities that misrepresented their official purpose. They should, however, not be seen as singing from the same hymn sheet with the colonial administrators and merchants.

Explaining why Christianity had been singled out for criticisms by a lot of nationalists for being the agent of *underdevelopment* and *exploitation* of Africa, S.G. Williamson, opined that the other agencies that spread Western influence - political, commercial economic and social, were expressed in terms of impersonal forces impinging upon traditional culture. The Church, (Christianity) is an institution whose impact, personalised in its missionaries and agents, is a target for attack as an enemy in personal form. Through the missionaries, the Church had a close contact with Africans. It appeared in their villages, entered their homes, educated their children and buried their dead. The Church, displaced the traditional religion, permeated and disrupted every aspect of the local culture. *The Church is a personal intruding force, making known its requirements, disciplining its membership...*

> *Its voice has been heard speaking personally to family and to individual and its influence had been directly experienced. It is the institution that they know and recognise as the agent of change. Again, the Church came as a bearer of spiritual values as concerned with man and his destiny.*[10]

The Western Christian missionary impact had been wrongly seen by nationalist writers as the concomitant of the total Western impact in its religious and humanitarian aspects upon African **undislocated** traditional world and society. This stems from the 19th century European ideal of redeeming Darkest Africa from its barbarism by the application, through government and religion of Western civilisation and the Christian religion.

Despite the extreme nationalist criticism of Christianity, its close contact with humanity's real needs and aspirations was responsible for its great contributions to the progress of humanity in the world. Its light has been shining in several places in Africa. Christianity is an agent of progress and development in human society and its personal touch with human basic needs makes it vulnerable and open to undeserved attack. As a *transforming agent*, it does not spare any institution or element that hinders human development as well as movement to the attainment of total *freedom and progress*. No single factor has contributed more to human and societal progress in Africa than Christianity. Consequently, the nationalists would criticise it more for what they called *destruction of traditional cultural patterns of African development.*

Many believe that development manifested by the presence of Christianity, education and colonialism is a radical revolutionary change, which is cataclysmic, and a break with tradition. Development is seen to take a negative stance against tradition because of a commitment to destroy the old order so as to build the new. Agents of development do not aim at balance of powers but at a total defeat of the traditional structure and planting a new one. The apathy, fatalism and constricted outlook typical of traditional societies are supplanted by a more optimistic, wide-ranging view of life. Thus the basic platform of change is a frontal attack on tradition in order to implant a new ideology.[11]

Some nationalists feel that this view is wrong. It is not entirely wrong. Some traditions must be eradicated if a *step-forward* must be taken. We must break completely with a *negative* past if a *positive* future must be stepped into. This is the radical stance of the missionaries. Some modest revolutionaries hold the view that in an encounter between Christianity and African traditions in some societies, traditions are not seen as necessarily being opposed to development. They believe that development could come by utilising favourable elements in the traditions in order to change the unfavourable ones. Traditions could mediate between the agents of development and the acceptance of development.

Tradition to them could be a means of *domesticating* the forces development - a control that keeps development within the goals of *humanisation*. In other words, it will keep development within the limits of human needs and benefits. A dynamic relationship exits between tradition and *development* in two dimensions. Development cautiously places tradition under the anvil, and critically appraises its viability in solving human progress in its confrontation with nature. By this, there is no place for romantically clinging to a tradition when it becomes a dead wood. Similarly, a worthwhile tradition that is productive and constructive should not be thrown away for any reason at all.

At present, various African communities strongly stress the importance of combining developments with traditional values to make them meaningful, relevant and profitable to people's existential needs. Development (as currently understood and applied in some quarters), particularly in Community Development Projects going on in many communities in Africa, implies introducing desirable changes in rural communities among people who still live without basic modern amenities of life. Such communities that live *closest to nature* are being made to see the need for improved water supply, all-season good roads, good medical care within the closest neighbourhood, good houses, affordable all-year round food supply, good education for the children, etc. Many African societies south of Sahara lack all of these basic amenities in their communities. Smart politicians, therefore, see them as political campaign issues and use them as mere gimmicks to win votes from the illiterate towns people and villagers. Basic human rights and needs are often termed *luxuries and privileges* in many rural communities in Africa. Consequently, either from social, personal, cultural or political as well as technological levels, many people in the West still see Africa and her peoples as *under-developed*.

The notion of development is a complex one and as such has been understood in different ways by different people. The politicians, for instance, would see it as *political stability and institutionalisation of political goals and means of achieving them.*[12] It is seen as increased differentiation and specialisation of political structures and culture. The economists, on the other hand, would see national development to mean *the number of industries… capital formation… a nation has attained within* a given time.[13] Those who see it from the perspective of social development and progress as we have earlier stated, place emphasis on *institutionalisation* of Western social norms and behaviour patterns. This involves transformation of inherited traditional artefacts. Since it is a complex phenomenon, it can be seen from the level of individual as increased skill and capacity, greater freedom, creativity, self-discipline, responsibility and material well-being. At the level of a social group, it would imply in addition, increased capacity to regulate both internal and external relations. This will mean that nations are in close transactions and the possession of the ability of the individual members to regulate them to the benefit of the whole country.

This is a situation where every individual knows his or her privileges and responsibilities and works hard and diligently for the common good.

On the other hand, G. Onibonoje sees development as understood by many people in Africa today to mean larger and fuller growth in human endeavours in the positive sense.[14] Probably, he is emphasising that both human and social aspects of the concept are needed if the emergent nation-states in Africa are really going to be *developed*. However, it must be emphasised here that development as he understood it should not start with *goods* but rather with *people* and the education, organisation and the discipline that guide the use of the goods.

From the fore- going, one can deduce that Africa is still facing the problem of *under-development*. Africans are still living in poverty, hunger and disease due to either ignorance or superstition or both. Africans, by the level of their technological growth in modern time, cannot effectively combat ecological problems threatening the continent in several places and ways- drought, desert encroachment, flood, soil-erosion, oil spillage, volcanic eruption, among others. Low level of food production cannot serve a fast -growing population. Africa is thus not meeting up with her socio-economic needs because of lack of technical know-how in addition to a number of other factors. The cause of this inability should no longer be blamed on outside forces. We shall now start to look for some explanations from within. One of the ways of doing it, is by analysing some factors that affect people's thought pattern and action. Thus, the traditional religion and culture, which *control, predict* and *explain space-time events* in Africa, should be critically examined to assess their viability in the light of Africa's past experiences and her present situation.

1.2   African Traditional Religion and Culture

The oldest form of religion and culture found in Africa by the early Arab and European travellers and visitors was neither Christianity nor Islam. In this work, we shall use the term *African Traditional Religion and Culture* for the original and indigenous religious and cultural genre practised in the continent ere the arrival of missionary religions: Christianity and Islam. Those early Arab and European travellers and merchants were shocked to meet a form of religion so diametrically different from the ones they knew in their own countries.

They out of sheer ignorance and prejudice resorted to use all sorts of derogatory terms to describe the religion. Invariably, the religious system was intricately related to the people's culture and traditions. It was the basis of their understanding and perception of the universe.

In this text, we shall use tradition to mean the cultural traits, which persist through a considerable life span. The word comes from the Latin root *tradio,* meaning something handed down from one generation to the other. Traditions imply values, belief, rules and behaviour-patterns that are shared by a group of people and passed on from one generation to another as part of socialisation process. Tradition provides a society with its cosmology, explains the nature of things, their origin and being and even the future destiny of the universe.[15]

The notion of tradition presupposes another social concept- culture. Scholars had adopted some descriptive, practical and functional approaches in their attempt to explain and interpret the meaning and significance of culture in people's lives. The eminent British anthropologist, Sir E. B. Tylor, who introduced the term into Social Sciences in the 19th century defined it *as that complex whole which included knowledge, beliefs, art, morals, customs and any other capabilities and habits acquired by man as a member of society.*[16] In more recent past, J.H. Fichter, defined it as *the total configuration of institutions that the people in society share in common.*[17] Paul R. Mussen *explains* culture to mean that *body of stored knowledge, characteristic way of thinking and feeling, attitudes, goals, and ideals.*[18] Many other definitions abound, all emphasising its peculiarity to a people that own it.

There is a close relationship between *culture* and *tradition* as can be deduced from the views of the scholars expressed above. It is pertinent to remark that tradition seems to be a subject of culture. In other words, we can speak of the tradition of marriage or inheritance as part of the entire cultural system of a people. Culture therefore, embraces more than tradition. It includes a people's way of life, a reflection of their distinctive characteristics and peculiarities, their value orientation, world -view, institutions and achievements in the various fields of human activities- legal, literary, artistic, scientific, religious, philosophical and technological aspects of life.[19]

It is necessary here to say a little more on culture and its features especially as they affect this work. We still do not know much about the origin of cultures because of its obscurity in antiquity. The little we can be sure of may be derived from research results carried out in many other cultural systems. In general principles, it is now obvious that human cultural development covers vast period in human history. Throughout most of that time, social change has certainly been unnoticed slow and often steady. However, in some parts of Africa, the rate of change bas been rapidly accelerated in recent years. Change in culture is inescapable and inevitable because no society is static. The factors making for stability and those making for change are both inherent aspect of culture. New cultural elements can arise within a cultural system.

This feature is better described as *invention*. It may come from some other cultures through the process of *diffusion*. Invention inevitably involves the use of existing cultural elements in some new combinations. Therefore, the larger the cultural base, other things being equal, the greater the wealth of elements from which new inventions can be fashioned. This applies to both cultural objects and to ideas. Most of the inventions represent minor modifications or changes in the details of the culture. The basic pattern of the society is less frequently or radically modified. The eventual effects of inventions are so far-reaching that it is almost impossible to envisage in advance what aspects of a culture will be changed by some given innovation. The determining factor in the integration of a new artefact or thought-pattern (ideas) into a culture is how the new items fit into the prevailing scheme. No trait is intrinsically of high or low value. It always comes to be evaluated in terms of standards prevailing on the culture, the standards themselves of course, having been innovations originally.

Having seen the relationship between *tradition and culture*, it is almost pertinent to evaluate that between *religion* and *culture*. Both religion and culture (particularly in Africa), are inseparable part of a corpus of human life. Their inter-relatedness is such that it is impossible for a society to have one without the other. Although both are inter-related, we must state that their autonomy is not contested. Consequently, Zunni has maintained that no culture has appeared or developed except together with a religion. Consideration of religion as a culture product is therefore only comprehensible in the sense that every culture and religion possess each other in such a way that every culture possesses a religious sense and vice versa. But this does not mean that culture and religion are one and the same thing.[20] This notion should be clear in the mind of any one interested in field work in Africa because some informants and field assistants might tend to confuse the two systems. For instance, each ingredient of culture in Africa makes sense within the total context of that culture.[21] In every analysis of data collected through fieldwork, religion of the Africans illuminates the traditional culture of the people who possess it just in the same way that the same religion finds its expression in the cultural system. It is this religion, which has been immersed in the cultural system and has found its expression in it that has also *directed, controlled* and *shaped* the system of life, pattern of thought and behaviour.

The entire system of African life is to a large extent, the product and function of *African Traditional Religion*. This religion which has affected and influenced every aspect of African life is the religion we have described and defined as *African Traditional Religion and Culture*. It is a part of the culture, which *incorporates the traditions of the people who use it to validate the cultural norms and practices and express their word-views*. African cosmology is strongly propped in religious factor. Invariably, African development and underdevelopment are underpinned by the religious beliefs and practices.

What Africa is today is more of the product and impact of their traditional religion than any other factor that has impacted on them. Although the early foreign visitors and writers who pioneered the study of African Traditional Religion described it with all sorts of derogatory terms, it is evident that the form of religion they found was not a revolutionary and missionary faith like Christianity, full of enthusiasm for mission and progress. This ancestral faith erroneously daubed *heathenism, fetishism, idolatry, savage, paganism, primitive, juju,* etc. by the foreign writers controlled every aspect of African life but could not usher in a type of socio-economic development that could have steadily moved on to other parts of the world as model for people to copy. The present problem of underdevelopment can be traced to the nature and functions of this traditional religion that did not actually explore ways and means to establish sustainable economy that could have stood the test of time. The type of culture nurtured and sustained by this traditional religion could not resist the onslaught of the invading external agents of change. It is still doubtful if the attempts being made by educated African elite to revive the traditional cultures and religion could turn Africa into a leading manufacturing and industrialised society in the 21ˢᵗ century. Nor could it help to establish lasting democracy in every country in the continent where living standard of the ordinary people would be enhanced.

From the view point of our interest in developing a modern Africa, perhaps the most important aspect of traditional cultures is the elaborate ideology of supporting the system of government.

Clearly associated with this, is the veneration of the land, often elaborated in religious rituals, which underlie the system of land tenure and the limitation of its use and *sale* as a factor of production. Another element that has particular significance for modern life is the *veneration* or *worship* of ancestors, which reinforces the bond of kinship and the importance of clans and lineage. From this, it can be seen that changes in economic structure and political organisation often involve questions of religious beliefs.[22] We shall in the second part of the book, show from available data how these cardinal religious beliefs and practices affect self-sufficiency. Invariably, the historical problem, *under-development* could be traced to these religio-cultural factors which were unable to produce sustainable development in the continent of Africa.

NOTES

1. Gustavo Guturez   *A   Theology   of Liberation.* London: SCM Press, 1974, p. 24.

2. H. Jaguaribe   *Economic and Political Developments: A Theoretical Approach and Brazilian Case Study.* (Cambridge: Harvard University Press) 1968.p 4. Reprinted, 1990

3. G. Myrdal   What is Development? *Journal of Economic Issues* Vol. 8,4 (1974), pp. 729- 739.

4. Walter Rodney   How Europe Underdevelopment Africa.(London: Bogle Le Ouverture Publications, 1972), p. 9

Cf. R.I. Rhodes,(ed)   *Imperialism and Under-development: A Reader.* (NY. Monthly Review Press, 1970)

5. E.C. Amaucheazi   The Problem of National Development in E.C. Amaucheazi (ed.) *Readings in Social Sciences.* Enugu-Nigeria, Fourth Dimension Publisher, 1980,) p. 9. Revised 1998.

6. D. L. Johnson   *The Sociology of Change and Reaction in Latin America.* (New York) 1973, p. 6

7. N. Ashcraft   *Colonisation and Underdevelopment.* NY, 1973, p. 6

cf. B. Berberoglu   The meaning of Underdevelopment: A critique of Mainstream Theories of Development and Underdevelopment. *Quarterly Journal of School of International Studies.* 17, 1, (Jan- March, 1978), pp 55 ff

8. W. Rodney   ibid. 227

9. Aylwald, Shorter,   *African Christian Theology.* London Geoff. Chapman, 1975, p. 22

10. S. G. Williamson   *Akan Religion and Christian Faith.* (Accra Ghana: University Press (1965 p. 153. Reprinted E.J. Brill, 1994

11. O.U. Kalu   Tradition in Revolutionary Change. *Ikenga, Journal of African Press,* Vol. 3, nos. 1 & 2, (1975), p. 55

12. O. Nnoli   *Path to Nigerian Development.* (Darkar: Cordsria), 1981, p. 29. Revised and Reprinted 1994.

13. O. Nnoli   ibid., p. 29

14. G.O. Onibonoje   *The Indigenous for National Development* (Ibadan Nigeria: Longmans Group, 1976), p. 137

15. Hunter & Winter (eds.)   *Encyclopaedia of Anthropology.* (NY, Harper & Row, n.d.), p. 138

16. E.B. Tylor,   *Primitive Culture,* Vol. 1 (London, 1871), p. 21. Reprinted, 1994

17. J.H. Fihter   *Sociology.* Chicago: Univ. of Chicago Press, 1957, p. 270

18. P.H. Mussen   *The Psychological Development of the Child.* N.J., 1963, p. 62.

19. Broon, Selznick   *The Principles of Sociology.* NY., 1970, PP 50 - 51. Reprint, 1993.

20. G. Zununi   *Man and His Religion: Aspects of Religious Psychology.* (London, 1969), p. 145, Reprinted and Enlarged, 1995.

    Cf. F. Bractlett,   Religion as Experience, Belief and Action in *Riddel Memorial Lectures* (London: Oxford University Press), p. 3

21. Ruth Benedict   *Patterns of Culture.* New York: Menthor Books, 1959, p. 207, 2nd Ed. 1989

22. W. Goldschmidt   Culture and Changing Values in Africa, in W. Goldschmidt, (ed.) *The United States and Africa.* (London and New York: F.Praeger Inc. 1963, pp 193 - 194, Reprinted, 1996.

CHAPTER TWO
Early European Ideas of Africa

It is important to give a brief review of the old accounts of European contact with Africa, and how the impressions and views of the early visitors affected policies and actions in Africa. That will help those who either might have forgotten that aspect of African history or have not studied it at all. The initial contact influenced the views but with time, such views determined what later travellers wanted to see even when such things had changed or never existed. This aspect of African history has long been deleted from the syllabuses of schools in many African countries and might be the same with schools in many parts of the world. Besides, this background story throws more light on the main thrust of this work. Those early contacts and views expressed by the visitors including travellers, explorers, missionaries, anthropologists and colonial administrators, left long-term and far-reaching impressions that directed the formulation of cultural and administrative policies in the colonies. It is important, therefore, to look at a few of them again.

2.1   Early Contact with Africa

We are using contact with West Africa as an illustrative model. It speaks for what happened in some other places, although each sub-region has its own peculiar reports and descriptions by those who visited there. It is not going to be a detailed analysis of the history of the period. Reference will be made to other parts of Africa when it is necessary to use them to validate our viewpoints. The focus is West Africa, and it will be a representative case study.

Before the second half of the 15th century, many Europeans knew little or nothing about Africa, South of Sahara. For long, many people remained ignorant of events and ways of life in Africa unless those gleaned from distorted accounts by travellers and writers eager for the exotic. Even the little the Europeans knew came from occasional Arab travellers who lacked the appropriate tools of language to understand African ways of life and thought. Some of the few Arab travellers and geographers who visited the continent of Africa did not make many inroads into the hinterlands. As far back as the time of Herodotus in the 9th century, it was reported that King Necho of Egypt sent out an early expedition led by Pheonician mariners. The expedition probably sailed from the Red Sea and later returned to Egypt and could not go further south.

The French had on the other hand, claimed to have discovered the Gold Coast in 1346, over a century earlier than the recorded Portuguese arrival. The French claims went further to state that they established and maintained a regular trade for many years before the El Mina Fort was destroyed by fire in 1694. The French Admiral of the Fleet from whose records we obtained these facts, claimed that he had anchored at Dieppe and Rouen. The Portuguese account and other sources have seriously challenged the French claim, which stated that:

> in 1683, French Traders erected the first shore establishment in Africa near the mouth of the Senegal River... in 1678 the French Government also acquired from the Dutch the offer-shore Island of Gore near Cape Verde which became their base...[1]

John Barbot, an eminent slave trader who was a Huguenot before coming to England served as an Agent of the Royal Company of Africa that shipped slaves to the New World. He did not believe the French claim and openly declared his total rejection of the same. According to him,

> if this account be true, it is strange that no mention is made of it by other French historians... particularly De Sarres and Mezroy. Such considerable undertaking and so rich a trade seemed to deserve a place in history...The silence of French historians in this point is just cause to suspect the validity of the author's assertions; nor do I find in history of Portugal, which is so full of Portuguese discoveries of Nigritia and Guinea, the least mention of their having heard of any French men that had founded the Castle of Mina in 1384 and began there his first entrenchment ever saw or heard such Castle built by French an hundred years before [2]

Many other criticisms against French claim came up at the same time. However, the most reliable and authentic account of voyages of discovery that made lasting contact was that pioneered by the Portuguese under the patronage of their brave and courageous Prince Henry the Navigator. It was Portugal that took the lead in the series of adventure to open contacts with Africa. In spite of the suspected monsters and evil spirits that were reported to haunt the unknown seas around the Equator, the Portuguese vessels broke the ice and got as far as the Bight of Benin in 1472. A Portuguese mariner, Diago Cao also carried his ships to the estuary of the River Congo.

Bartholomew Diaz and Vasco Da Gama passed the Cape of Good Hope and went towards the East in search of spices and other articles of trade. By 1485, John D'Alveiro visited Benin in Nigeria and it was reported that soon after that, trade began on ivory and pepper in exchange for European products. This continued till the demand for slaves from West Africa in the New World outstripped the demand for other commodities. These initial contacts were primarily commercial and the Portuguese Crowns exercised close control over the trade, for by virtue of Papal Bulls, the Portuguese Kings claimed the whole of West African coast as their exclusive sphere of influence and authority.[3] However, Henry the Navigator, who was described as a pious and religious monarch, included both the propagation of the Christian Faith and the discovery of the kingdom of the legendary Prester John in his scheme. The news of this **Utopian Kingdom** existing somewhere in Africa had circulated in Europe for long and people wanted to discover and establish contact with it.

A.F.C. Ryder has argued that by the 1530s, the Portuguese control of the West African coastal trade began to crack and dwindle under the strain of their increasing worldwide commitments. The growing pressures from other rivals especially France and England who could not recognise the Portuguese monopoly of the lucrative trade that flourished worsened this. The Portuguese, nevertheless, maintained their dominant power on the coast for another century till a new maritime power, the Dutch, established rival fortified posts, beginning with Fort Nassau in 1612. Thereafter, other Europeans struggled to register their presence and influence along the Coast of West Africa, either as individuals on their own under the auspices of their countries' patronage or as emissaries of other foreign powers and as trading companions too.

The exploration of the hinterlands especially the River Nile down East and Central Africa came later. The efforts of David Livingstone and Cecil Rhodes in that respect had been very outstanding and rewarding. Briefly stated, the opening of African interior by explorers, geographers and other travellers was an adventure that had economic interest as its primary objective; religious factor came much belatedly. The 18th century revivalism in England was the principal factor that prompted and hastened the pace of mission outreach to Africa.

2.2   Views about West Africa and her Religion and Culture

As already indicated, some of the earliest visitors to Africa were Arab traders and geographers who entered through the North African routes. Although the traders were primarily engaged in commercial activities, they did not leave off propagation of their religion at certain periods when they came into close contacts with Africans especially at the courts of the rich and ruling kings. One of the celebrated Arab travellers was Ibn Battuta. His journey from the northern fringes of Africa to the old Empires of the Western Sudan preceded the Portuguese entry through the sea between the 14th and 16th centuries. Thomas Hodgkin had hailed the accounts of those early travellers and geographers as important because

> *they cover period roughly from the 8th to 15th centuries during which there was no knowledge of and no account.. West* Africa.[4]

So those early accounts, though cursory and lurid, covered a missing gap. For instance, Ibn Battuta and his group were interested in certain practices that excited them, particularly the cannibalism which they glaringly described as the main feature of the religion and culture of the Blacks they met in the region. He claimed that some blacks told him that the tastiest meat in the flesh of women were the palms and the breasts.[5] The cannibal story seemed to have been widespread in Europe at some time later. For instance, Cavazzi's description of the Kingdom of the Congo, Motamba and Angola, gave prominence to cannibalistic practices in the territory. The artist of a fine quarto volume, which was published in 1678 gave a vivid expression to this popular belief in Europe at the time. He clearly presented and portrayed a picture of a cannibal scene in which several Angolans were butchering human limbs and cooking them in grid iron.[6] Africans, on the other hand, seemed to hold similar view of Europeans as being cannibals. For instance, John Barbot had once remarked that among the Africans his company shipped to America as slaves, were

> *many … who were positively prepossessed with the opinion that we transport*
> *them into our country in order to kill them… and believed the Europeans to*
> *be great and irresistible cannibals.*[7]

Similarly, Captain Theodore Canot, another outstanding slave dealer, criticised the barbaric and brutal treatment which the slaves received in the hands of their captors and those who transported them.[8] He concluded that such was sufficient for the slaves to conclude that their white captors were heartless cannibals. So the cannibal saga was common in both camps. Condemning Africans as cannibals, the Europeans described African religion and culture with such grotesque and lurid language that would titillate those eager for the exotic. This was really a reflection of the milieu in which they lived. Those who described the religion and culture found in different parts of the continent where they sojourned used derogatory language, which pointed to their ignorance of the system. Some of them were not believers in religion at all back home in their country and as such showed no respect to any form of religion they met in Africa. Some others made outright comments that depicted prejudice and hatred because of their own religion, which they compared with the type they met. A few of such views will suffice to illustrate the general impression and magnitude of the visitors' arrogance and ignorance of the religious and cultural system they met in Africa.

Duarte Pecheco Pereira (1505 - 1520) describing the religion of the Africans living between Rio Formosa along the Guinea Coast stated that:

> *there are lots of wrongful usage in the way they live … I shall not speak of*
> *their fetish and idols…. The Negroes are idolatrous. We shall avoid*
> *mentioning them.*[9]

In R. Halluyt's ***Principal Navigation***, we have a list of European travellers who were by mid 1550s able to come as near as El Mina and Benin. They also picked up interest in the religion and culture of the Negroes and made their own impressions known. Such men included the Dutch sailor called D.R. whose full names and identity were still unknown. Probably he might be a medical doctor who accompanied the early travellers. His title *Dr.* might have been mistaken to be a name or his initials and this featured in most documents that bore the records he put down in his journals and diaries. This view of D.R. has not been validated with any other document elsewhere. Other visitors included Peter de Marees, de Bry and Pinteado. Dr. F. D' Olfert Dapper came a century later in about 1688 when a new breakthrough had been made in the Sciences. Yet his own opinion did not differ much from those of his predecessors. The period was an era of great rush and intensive scramble for areas of commercial interest in Africa and many European countries wanted to register their presence and authority in any part of the continent they could hold firm. Many of those travellers made some devastating, (how be it, honest to them,) remarks. For instance:

> ... *a confused mass of ridiculous superstitions (D'Elbe); a world of superstitious customs(Snelgrave); a king of idolatry of an unbelievable absurdity(Prunlau de Pomergeorge); so ridiculous as such a mess they profess to worship both god and devil whom they sacrifice men and cattle* (Dapper)[10]

John Barbot whom we have mentioned earlier, did not paint a better picture either. To him, the religion and culture was:

> *a gross superstitious paganism, though most of them acknowledge a Supreme Being, but in a every erroneous manner...Being thus prepossessed, they turn their thought and practices to those absurd inferior gods in whom they put their confidence.*[11]

Although Barbot knew the Coast of West Africa better than most of his predecessors or colleagues who travelled at the same time with him, his impressions of the Negroes was in no way positive.

He could have given a balanced and objective view of what prevailed as he observed them but to him the Africans were:

> *extremely sensual, knavish, revengeful impudent liars, impertinent, gluttonous , extravagant... so intemperate that they drink brandy as if it were water; deceitful in their dealings with Europeans... rob and commit murders on high ways... the blacks are so dextrous and expert in stealing that they will rob an European before his face without being perceived by him...*[12]

Earlier on, Captain J. Welsh, an explorer and naval officer who was in the coast of West Africa at the same time with Dapper around 1688 had tactlessly and carelessly declared that Africans were people of

> *beastly living, without God, laws, religion and commonwealth.* [13]

Captain Welsh probably made his observations from Benin where he spent most of his time and compared Benin with the Europe he knew back at home. He obviously failed to notice that a century earlier, Portuguese missionaries who visited Benin reported that they met a well-established and organised Kingdom ruled by a monarch who was so powerful that they took the news home to King John II of Portugal (1481 - 1495) who in turn sought to open friendly correspondence with the Benin Monarch. The missionaries saw the *Oba* (King of Benin) as one who occupied a higher post in his domain than the Pope did in Catholic Europe. His subjects saw the Oba not only as God's Vice-regent on earth but also as a god himself.[14] The African monarch who ruled large empires commanded a lot of respect from his subjects. It is not yet confirmed that the Benin Empire had declined so badly by the time Captain Welsh visited about a century later, that he could not notice signs of organised state and imperial authority; which the missionaries saw and praised. If the Old Benin Empire was still in existence when Welsh visited, he was probably comparing it with what he knew of European empires and domains. Granted that Benin Kingdom did not meet with Welsh's ideas of Kingdoms in Europe, it was unfair and unrealistic to deny that such empire ever existed, however small or ill-developed. Besides, the *annals of Missionary journals* reported of many religious rituals and ceremonies in the empire of Benin they met. In fact a form of Catholic faith was established in Benin, which existed for a short time and died off from the persecution it received from votaries of Traditional Religion in Benin.

William Bosman, the Chief Factor of the Dutch Company at El Mina had no good impression of Africa of his own day. A shrewd businessman deeply involved in Slave Trade, Bosman was surprised to see many Africans who were not only as corrupt as he was but also smart enough to outwit and dupe him on several occasions.

His nasty experience in West Africa made him conclude that:

> *the Negroes are still without exception crafty villainous, and fraudulent and very seldom to be trusted. Being sure to slip no opportunity of cheating any European or indeed one another. A man of integrity is as rare among them as a white falcon... for they seem indeed to be born and bred as villains.*

On the religion proper, Bosman felt that

> *it is more to be lamented that the Negroes idolise such worthless nothings by reason that several among them have no... idea of the Deity.*

Similarly, religious artefacts meant nothing to him. The Africans in their obtuse state of mind,

> *cry, let us make fetiche, by which they express as much as let us perform our religious worship.*[15]

William Bosman who was deeply involved in the nefarious Slave Trade was bold enough to talk of integrity and honesty as a way of life. Probably his understanding of the terms was different!

The above were a sample of the numerous derogatory remarks about Africa and her culture made by some of the early European visitors and writers. They were published in numerous books and magazines in Europe and consequently, influenced many minds who uncritically believed them. It took time to correct some of the views though many still hold them to be valid and unchanging. It is sad that some current events in contemporary Africa seem to justify these early negative remarks!

The 15th and 16th centuries in Europe were the *age of explorations and discovery*. Europe had discovered a new continent - the Americas, rounded the Cape of Good Hope, established trading posts and military bases in the Persian Gulf and Indian Ocean. The views expressed by those travellers, merchants or explorers were not comprehensive accounts of the faith of the people or a systematic study of the traditional religious beliefs prevalent in Africa then. They were loose stands of information, which appeared weird and exotic and probably impressed those who heard them. Each reporter picked what impressed him and most of the time; it would be aspects of the culture and religion that were ridiculous, absurd or repulsive. African culture was thought to be subsumed in religion which was seen in those early days as the main preoccupation of the *primitive minds*. Hence the early European visitors were the first to give the religious vocabulary that erroneously described African Traditional Religion and that vocabulary had unfortunately persisted in some quarters. For instance, cult objects like *charms, amulets, mascots* found in Africa were described as *feticho*.

The Portuguese visitors who gave those religious artefacts the pejorative names had similar objects at home but did not use them for religious purposes. Others who followed them later spelt it in their own way and confused the whole religious system with such wrong terminology. Other wrong terms that have persisted in religious books include heathenism, *paganism, idolatry, savage, native, juju, etc.* E.B Idowu has carefully dismissed these, as inadequate expressions and descriptions of a long established religious system that has stood the test of time 16. Many modern writers and scholars have discarded the use of some of the terms as inadequate to describe African Traditional Religion and Culture.

2.2.1 *Background to the views*

It is helpful to discuss some of the antecedents that led to the views expressed by early European visitors to Africa. The traditional religion was fascinating and in fact exciting and often puzzling. Although those foreigners lacked the tools to study the religion they met, many of them who wanted to understand it resorted to present it in such a way that it might excite those at home in Europe. Their main concern was primarily centred of how to expose the *errors* and *absurdity* of the theology of the religion and the *barbarism* of its rituals and practices. This was particularly true of the Christian missionaries who used such methods to raise funds for their work among the *heathens* they were trying to *evangelise.* This led Thomas Hodgkin to infer that although those visitors failed to understand the traditional religious systems, at the same time... they were interested in...

> *those aspects of African cultures which judged from the standpoint of their own cultural assumption were especially odd , ridiculous or repellent.*[17]

Among the writers of the period of Portuguese commercial ascendancy on the Coast of West Africa from the 15th century to the middle or the end of the 16th century, were court officials, who wanted to project the standpoint of the regime. That included the expansion of the Portuguese trade in slaves, pepper, the diffusion of Portuguese culture and winning African souls for the Catholic Faith. To achieve all these, the visitors had to paint a picture of horror which will justify their mission and presence. It was an age when European expansion was gaining ground in many parts of the world. Trading posts were being established alongside missionary outstations. For instance, missionaries and merchants were sent to China and Japan and traders who accompanied them occupied themselves with surveys of business opportunities. The merchants benefited from the riches found along their routes and at their destinations. The material foundation of Western civilisation was firmly secured in that century.

The 17th century Europe is known as the century of genius. Modern science was born in that age. That was preceded by the Dark Ages several centuries earlier and had obviously dawned into the Age of Renaissance- an age of awareness, an era of Humanism when man felt that he had come of age. The traditional outlook of medieval Christianity concerning the universe was radically altered and the old value system was critically and radically challenged.

The great scientific discoveries and achievements of men like Copernicus, (died 1543), Kepler, Galileo, Rene Descartes, Newton, etc. had a profound impact on the mental outlook of the Western man. Rene Descartes invented analytical geometry, developed a theory of light. His division of the world into mind and matter enabled him to say that the material world was the proper sphere of scientific investigations unhampered by religious interference. He made one of the most influential attempts of the time to determine the relationship between religion and science.

Until the middle of 17th century, Western civilisation had been basically Christian. There had been no specific challenge to Christian concepts of the *Universe*. But suddenly, the revolutionary developments in sciences severed the ties binding the West to its Christian past and articulated basic concepts of modern secular world-view. The discoveries (as already stated) encouraged a general belief that there were no mysteries that human intellect could not resolve. The numerous criticisms and insults on African Traditional Religion and Culture were a reflection of the growing tendency of rationalists' opposition to religion in general. So anti-religious feelings and expressions made by some of those early Europeans who found themselves in Africa were reflections of their feelings against religion, particularly Christianity in Europe. The views of the religious people and organisations against African religion were based on a different ground, particularly that of prejudice and culture shock and spiritual pride.

One of the greatest critics of the Bible and Christianity at that period was Baruch Spinoza (1637 - 1677). He suggested in very strong and uncompromising terms, the elimination of all *traditional beliefs* and all organised religions and clearly expressed his disbelief in miracles and the Supernatural. By *traditional beliefs*, Spinoza did not mean African Traditional Religion and Culture, but the religious traditions which the West was accustomed to and on which her civilisation had long been established. He stated that God had no existence outside the world. There is no doubt that this type of intellectual climate influenced many of the people including Christians who came to Africa and looked down on the traditional religion and culture of the people.

By early 18th century, the secularisation of Western Europe had begun to spread far and wide. *Reason* was then seen as the only infallible guide to knowledge. The intellectuals of the period called it the *Age of Enlightenment* - an enlightenment that meant the rejection of any supernatural explanation of the universe. To some of them, *Religion* was seen as an instrument of exploitation devised (as Voltaire explained) by scoundrels to *prey on the ignorance of the masses.* Consequently, Voltaire, in a satire, succinctly described in his book, *Utopia, an imaginary world- El Dorado-* a city where there were no priests, no monks, no laws , no lawsuits, no prisons and where *Science and Logic* solved all human problems. Voltaire and the other rationalists consistently mocked religion and defied the existence of God. *The first divine,* according to him, was *the first rogue who met the first fool whom he confused with irrational fable.* Many Europeans of the time who were influenced by such anti-God philosophy and were perhaps able to get into different pats of the world, especially Africa, exhibited similar attitude towards the established religious systems they met. No part of Africa where the visitors found themselves was spared of their adverse and destructive criticisms of the religion and culture. For instance, Herbert Thomas, an enlightened English man of his age, was in South Africa and came back with a very poor and unbalanced account of his trip. He stated that in spite of his great search among the Hottentots in South Africa, there was no spark of knowledge of God anywhere. In his own words,

> *I have made all efforts… to discover some sparks of religion or knowledge of God, of heaven, hell, or immortality. I could not find anything that way; no place of worship, no day of rest, no order in nature , no blame, no truth, no ceremony in birth or burials, mere brutishness and stupidness wholly overshadowing them* .[18]

We are yet to know any group in Africa who are bereft of the knowledge of God in a continent where people are *notoriously religious* and can hardly live without their religion and ceremonies. However, it is important to state that it was not only the anti- God philosophers and rationalists of the period who cast aspersion on the Africans and their traditional religious and cultural systems. We had stated this fact earlier and noted that each group of critics of the system had its own reasons for doing so. For instance, some Christian missionaries who believed in God were rude and hostile to the African Traditional Religion and Culture for a long time but later a few began to show some signs of respect and sympathy to the system and humbly decided to understudy its principles. While the anti-God philosophers acted the way they did, on the ground of their unbelief, Christian missionaries felt that they held the only true knowledge of God. We shall come to this point presently, but meanwhile, the milieu under review needs a further comment.

By the end of the 18th century, it looked as if the rationalists had already overthrown religion and *dethroned God* from his exalted position in Heaven. A group of intellectuals, nonetheless, took side with Deism. As the *Age of Reason* dethroned or defied God and glorified *Humanism*, the capability of man to solve all his problems without recourse to external assistance or dependence, it made man the centre of focus and power. The *great prophets* of the age - the philosophers, including economists, political theorists and social reformers, in unison sang praises in honour of *Man* The optimism of the age was perhaps better proclaimed by Marquis de Cordercet, (1743 - 1794), described as one of the historically minded philosophers of the period. He was the philosopher who set forth a *theory of perfectibility* through steady accumulation of knowledge and the triumph of *Reason*. Unfortunately, he died in prison, perhaps by suicide, while trying to escape from Paris during the period of French Revolution. What an irony of life! a man who dethroned God and glorified himself could still die so miserably like a rat!

Out of the 18th century's general interest in intellectual and cultural progress, came a specialised concern with the progress of human development.- that is successive steps or stages by which mankind had passed to reach its present eminence.[19] As the 18th century was full of hope and optimism , the 19th century unfortunately turned out to be an age of controversy . This has been traced to the remarkable scientific, technical and material advances that had begun in Europe in the preceding 17th century. It accelerated in each of the following centuries and propelled its civilisation outward.

So the much publicised classification of nature in the 18th century was really begun in a subtle and unobtrusive way by Linnaeus who published in 1735, his thesis on the *Systems Naturae*.[20] Biologists building on this and at times independently, began to propound a system whereby they classified and arranged the whole order of nature in a rational pattern. Man was kept at the peak of the scale and further varieties of mankind, *Homo Sapiens*, arranged in descending order of superiority based simply on skin colour - white, red, yellow, and black. When in 1859, Charles Darwin published his work, *The Origins of Species*, and in 1871, his *Descent of Man*, his view was both controversial and revolutionary in the sense that it challenged the long-established traditional Christian doctrine of *Creatio ex Nihilo* and design. But it was more or less a follow-up to Linnaeus' earlier publication which did not circulate wide then. When data about human culture and society outside Europe were collected by those who were able to travel to other parts of the world, analysis of the information was left to a rather vague and still undifferentiated Social Sciences most often under the rubric of *Moral Philosophy*. This was mostly carried out by arm-chair theorists at home in Europe. Using Darwin's theory, the 19th century *social evolutionists* tried to propound a theory of progressive development generally. This theory was particularly used to establish the fact that the history of the development of the West was an illustrative evidence of the direction in which mankind as a whole would move.

In other words, Africa and other Third World nations should copy Western model of development if they would be classified with those on the path of *progressive and civilised* ladder. Thus, the sociologist Comte, took up the thesis of Charles de Brosses, which was later published by E.B Tyler and built up a theory of civilisation in a Unilinear *Process*.[21]

We know that African concept of time is *cyclical* and not *lineal*. The impact of *lineal process* of development on the relationship between Africa and the *developed* world was so immense that nearly every relationship was determined by how the West saw Africa as being at the last rung of the ladder of human progress and development. We shall come this later. The use of *comparative method* reassured the Western intellectuals of the *rightness of their own developmental process as a society or* rather the elements in their own society that were *modern* in contrast to those elements held to be retrograde. This was particularly made explicit when in 1851, Queen Victoria opened in London, the *Great Exhibition of works of Industries of all nation* which could be rightly called the *first of many World Fairs.* The fair was intended to show the world that through the *Industrial Revolution,* England, which had reached the apogee of civilisation, had become the *World's Workshop.* The *scientific study* of human society which had begun was based on the differentiation of skin colour as a distinctive emblem of high level of development in art, culture, science and even religion because according to some individuals, God had given *One, True Religion to the Whites.*[22] The religion of other races was regarded as both false and crude. Some others even held and propagated the view that God created human beings unequal and this inequality was a *divine design* to serve a particular purpose in his scheme. Since *whiteness* of skin was the mark of the highest race, the darker races especially the Negroes, would be inferior in the increasing order of their darkness. On this basis, and with no further evidences, Africans were put at the bottom of the *developmental scale.*

A School of Thought- *the Teleological School-* was definitely articulate in propagating the notion that God created the blacks inferior to the whites for a particular purpose- that of serving the whites. The blacks were purposely given strong backs, weak minds and placid disposition so that they could labour effectively under the supervision of their white masters. The interpretation of racism by the *Teleological School* went a step further than those of their contemporaries. Theirs had a tremendous influence on those who carried out the nefarious trade on human beings. As long as it was the blacks that were shipped to the New World to work in the plantations, it was in order because they were created for such purposes. Many Church leaders gradually accepted and propagated this obnoxious view and supported it.

But typical of the 19th century colonial administrative officers influenced by this notion, was Sir R. F. Burton. He was appointed the Vice -Consul in 1861 and was expected to live in the Island of Fernando Po. Unfortunately, he was away from the station most of the time because it was discovered that he did not like to live there. This was later deduced from most of his remarks about the place and its people. He sojourned many years in West Africa, yet did not see anything admirable about the people and their religion. According to him,

> *the religion is still at the rude dawn of faith- Fetishism and had rarely advanced to idolatry... He has never grasped the ideas of personal deity, a*

duty in life, a moral code, or a shame of lying... He rarely believes in a future
state of rewards and punishment, which whether true or not are indices of
human progress.[23]

Sir Burton's dislike of the Negroes often made him present a strong caricature of them especially the Freetown Creoles he met in Sierra Leone. When he visited Dahomey, (the present Benin Republic), what actually struck him was human sacrifice which he gave a religious interpretation to justify his view that the Negroes were still at the state of rude religious faith. He, however, did not mention the usual cannibalism which was projected by those who came before him. Although critical analysis of Burton's work is not the primary concern of this work, it is important to note that he was like an explorer who took Africa as his playground but uniquely placed it within a global framework of his creation.[24]

What was implicit in the views of the early European visitors, in the first three centuries of contact became explicit in the 19th century. For instance, it became obvious that the notion of Africa as a Dark Continent either as an expression of geographical ignorance or one of *religio-cultural* prejudice, was a 19th century invention . Cultural prejudices and racism became firmly entrenched in the policies and attitudes in this century and in a subtle way, determined, the administrative work in the colonies. The previous data collected by early travellers had by the 19th century been systematically analysed and streamlined by a group of intellectuals and presented Africans either as *awful savages or silly children.* It was only under Western paternalism that Africans could be shown the way to modernity and development.

The literature of the colonial period, Christian missions and merchants of the 19th century had a good deal in them about the stages of development involved in what was widely thought to be the process and course of social evolution to Western peaks. Besides the overwhelming indignation and contempt of Western attitudes, there were a few who showed some glimmerings of a better understanding of the situation at a particular point in time and to them we now turn as documented in the missionary account of Africa and her Traditional Religion and Culture.

2.2.2 The 19th Century Missionary Account of African Traditional religion and Culture

As already indicated, European assessment of their achievements in art, science and culture affected and encouraged their belief that God had given the only true religion to the Whites. That spirit of enlightenment had not dawned on the pagans afar off. We have earlier noted that even during the *Age of Enlightenment*, religion in one form or the other, was the most meaningful part of human existence. It is still remembered that among the explorers and merchants of the 15th or 16th centuries were zealous missionaries who saw the finger of God in their discoveries and conquests of nature as they sailed the oceans and crossed the deserts and forests. It became common practice that where ever they set their feet and hoisted their flag, they also set up the Cross. The civilisation that was later to grow materialistic did not lack missionary enthusiasm from the beginning.

After a brief period of apparent success of secularisation, the later part of 18th and early 19th centuries saw a religious reawakening spread throughout Western and Central Europe. This explains the beginning and spread of such religious movements as Pietism, Quakerism, Methodism, etc. From the same intellectual climate that prevailed, emerged two different schools, one tracing the origin of the whole human race to one source and the other which traced it to diverse sources. The Victorian English man, believing that England had reached the apogee of human development in culture, religion and science, was morally obliged to spread the same to those in utter state of helplessness, ignorance and darkness. In a subtle way, it bore the stamp of charity and obligation but beneath the obvious charity was a positive challenge to *Scientific Racism*. This challenge was manifested in an assumption of a sense of duty towards the *heathens and pagans*. The sense of duty and obligation was christened *The White Man's Burden and Manifest Destiny* to spread the European Religion, learning and civilization. Indirectly, Christianity became what they regarded as European Religion- a term that did not help the Catholicity of Christianity in any way. Christianity is a universal faith and any attempt by any racial group to make it its exclusive faith that could colonise another race that has the same right to it could be seen as an imposition. This became African experience of missionary Christianity which led to the rejection of it in many communities. Therefore pride of culture, civilization and art later became pride of religion. With this understanding, the missionaries who went out into the interior and stayed longer than other travellers and merchants, played up the religious question more than any other aspect of African culture. Africans who have equal claims to Christianity were not made to understand it as such and out of sheer nationalism and ignorance resisted the faith in order to preserve what they called their own traditional religion and culture.

African Traditional Religion and Culture received the worst onslaught from foreign visitors because it was perhaps the most conspicuous phenomenon in African life. Perhaps, it constituted the worst obstacle to the missionaries in their attempt to evangelise and to the colonial administrators who saw it as a power tool of resistance to the introduction of alien and foreign rule in the hinterlands. Some of the missionaries saw the traditional religion as the devil's agent that should be destroyed and be replaced with the Light of Christianity if Africans must move upwards from their low level in the *developmental scale*. Generally it was seen as the mystical source of power and backbone to the resistance to imposition of colonial rule. Each of the speculations was right in so far as the traditional religion was the u*nderpinner* of African cosmology. Incidentally, the natives were not found in a condition that could be described as superior to those of the visitors who were Christians. The initial iconoclastic attack of the cultural norms by early Christian missionaries was one of the factors that led to the resistance in some communities. Many of the votaries of African Traditional Religion who resisted the introduction of the new faith- Christianity- did not know that it was the major factor that actually transformed *the pagan Europe and* brought it *into the realm of development.*

Although it is important to remark that missionary account of traditional religion was different in some ways, the same idea of superiority was found in their writings. Often, the missionaries stayed longer at a particular location than the other European visitors. This gave them the opportunity to observe African life at a closer range than those who casually saw one or two rituals at a few centres and drew conclusions and thus painted larger than life pictures of the situation. This is illustrated in a discussion between Edwin W. Smith (an outstanding missionary to Africa) and Emil Ludwig (an eminent biographer). The Revd Edwin Smith had told Ludwig what the missionaries were doing in Africa and how Africans were responding positively and enthusiastically to the new teachings about God. Ludwig was perplexed to hear that and in an unguarded moment, exclaimed:

> *how can the untutored Africans conceive God….How can this be? Deity is a philosophical concept which savages are incapable of framing.*[25]

To him, Africans can never think of God let alone believing in Him. Yet to the Africans, God is a **reality** not a **concept**. Belief in the Supreme God was common in many African communities.

Furthermore, the longer stay by some missionaries at certain centres than some other Europeans might have been responsible for the greater number of literature from them than from other groups. In addition, the amount of literature might have been primarily due to the nature of missionary sponsorship and attitude at the Home Base. The missionary lived on charity, the voluntary contributions from missionary society at Home.

On the other hand, some other European travellers and administrators had other forms of sponsorship. If the missionaries in the field were to continue to carry on with their assignment in Africa, they had to be in touch with the Parent Body at the Home Base. Hence the continuous flow of information from the mission field. To attract sympathy and financial subscription, the missionaries would exaggerate how they were battling with demons in the land of benighted Africans. Philip D. Curtin has elsewhere criticised the missionaries for their bad attitude in exaggerating some of the experiences for pure sensationalism aimed at fund raising. According to him, some of the missionaries who went to the

> *pagans in the various parts of the Empire, wrote back in details to the Home Society. Those letters were collected and published in journals with wide circulation as a means of stimulating missionary subscription.*[26]

After reading such pathetic stories, any one who made contributions to support those working in pagan lands would have a feeling of a deep sense of vicarious participation in the righting of the wrongs and total eradication of paganism.

Besides, the general indignant and contemptuous attitudes and remarks of the Europeans of the period, there were some missionaries who showed some restraint in their reports. We have already mentioned Revd E. W. Smith. Despite longer stay in a place, some of the missionaries were linguists whose reports were narrowly confined to their professional specialities. This professional skill in languages might have affected the Revd J.F. Schon who was at Onitsha in Nigeria with Bishop Samuel Ajayi Crowther. Schon's ability to assess the Igbo of Nigeria whom he watched with keen interest made him conclude that

> *The Igbos are in their way a religious people. The word Tsiuku.... (God) is continually heard...Their notion of some of the attributes of the Supreme Being are in many respects correct and their manner of expressing them striking.*[27]

Schon could arrive at such conclusion after a close study of the language of the Igbo people which enabled him to penetrate their religious world. This is a subtle way in which the missionaries who were Africans by descent and Western by orientation and training approached the traditional religion and culture of the people. S.A. Crowther and T.B Freeman of Church Missionary Society and the Wesleyan Missionary Society respectively were Africans who worked with European colleagues as missionaries to the Africans. Perhaps because of their background or probably because of their knowledge of the local language, they experienced less culture-shock than most other Christian missionaries of their own generation. Their attitude was ambivalent some of the time, but often they depicted a real people with comprehensive way of life instead of the cardboard savages in the accounts of most of their western colleagues.

They at times compared Africans with Western standard in which they were trained and groomed and found their own people wanting and lagging behind. Probably, a clearer understanding of Biblical Theology made Abbe Bouche, a Roman Catholic missionary in Dahomey understand the traditional religion better than most of his colleagues. He was known as a learned theologian who applied the training in theology when studying foreign culture and religion. Part of his writings later showed a clearer and better analysis of the cult symbols than those of his other colleagues. According to him, it was not

> *mere materials that received the respects of the black: he directs them towards a higher Power, hence it cannot be said that Dahomean and Nago(Negro?) ... religion is really fetishism as the term is generally meant.*[28]

In the same vein, Thomas J. Bowen, an American Baptist Missionary who clearly understood the errors in Yoruba religion still found some correct interpretations of the Supreme Being in it. He clearly understood the rationale behind Yoruba belief in the Supreme Being and their notion of his justice and holiness which form their conception of His morality. Yet some other writers had denied the people any knowledge of God entirely. However, it is important to note that in spite of the general hasty condemnation of the traditional religion and culture, *there are a few who from their individual observations* expressed balanced views of their experiences pointing out some of the pitfalls and strengths of the system they met in Africa.

2.2.3   *Some African Nationalist Reactions*

Pride of race and culture, which characterised early European attitude to Africa, generated in the 19th century a spate of reactions from a number of Africans who had received Western Education. Many of them attended mission schools and embraced Christianity but gave it up in protest at a point in time when they noticed the constant European attack on African religions and culture. Among those early 19th century nationalists who defended both the Black Race and their culture were E Wilmot Blyden,
Abayomi Cole, Sir H.H. Johnston, J. Mensa- Saba, J. E. Casely Hayford, Mojola Agbebi (and Ekiti Baptist Pastor) and Bishop James Johnson whose book *Yoruba Heathenism*, has been described as the independent account on Ifa Divination by a Yoruba author.

These men, among others in their group, became the fore-runners of the later nationalist fighters for political independence during the hey-day of colonial administration in Africa. They might be accused of over-reaction at certain points but probably their approach was the only matching response to the vigorous campaign by Europeans to misrepresent African culture. Neither of the two extreme positions could be said to have got it right even though there were elements of truth in each. The method of presentation was important. We can assess the contributions of those early nationalists by taking a close look at one of them as typical of the rest. We turn to Blyden for this.

Edward Wilmot Blyden was relentless in propagating cultural revivalism. He was a brilliant West -Indian born Liberian Statesman. Born in 1832, Blyden emigrated to Liberia at the age of eighteen. He attended the Alexandrian High School in Monrovia and trained as a teacher and clergyman under Rev. D.A. Wilson. After studying theology, classics, geography and mathematics, he became a lay preacher in 1853, tutor in 1854 and was ordained a Presbyterian minister in 1858. He later succeeded D.A Wilson as Principal of Alexandrian High School. He emigrated to Sierra Leone where he became well-known as an author and had many hectic years of nationalist struggles before he died in Sierra Leone.[29]

His primary concern was to grapple with the fundamental problem of his race. In other words, he tried to dispel the lingering myth of European ideas of the inferiority of the Blacks and the superiority of the Whites. In his book, *Christianity, Islam and the Negro Race* (1887), Blyden argued that American Christianity was used as a tool by the upholders of Slave Trade and discrimination to further Negro submissiveness. As the cultural arrogance of the Europeans grew with years through out the 19th Century, so did Blyden's efforts in making the Africans not discard their time-tested and functional institutions grow. In his book *African Life and Customs*, (1908), Blyden made his most important and systematic defence of African culture. He was not opposed to African societies borrowing and incorporating any aspect of Western culture they considered useful and helpful into theirs but believed strongly that educated Africans should be protected from becoming unnecessarily ashamed of their cultures as a result of the arrogant ethnocentric attitudes of Europe to Africa.[30] He consistently defended African ways of life and thought and advised his fellow educated colleagues to encourage their people to be confident in themselves and in their culture. This vibrant resistance to European claims of superiority persisted till the agitation for political independence in the colonies began in full force. Many other nationalist writers who came after Blyden did not see kindly to European attitude to African culture. Although this is not a place to blame any of the two sides , it was natural for both to behave the way they did- one being shocked by an unfamiliar culture and the other standing strongly in defence of his identity and self-image. However, it was unfortunate that many of the nationalists broke away from the Christian Church, which had been on the vanguard of development. It is sad that they saw the Church as an agent of oppression and discrimination. The present work is of the view that if both sides had properly understood each other, they could have worked happily and used the inherent divine element in Christianity for the improvement and development of the Africans.

2.3   Analysis and Conclusion

The European presentation of Africa was full of unbalanced views. Consequently, there were cases of misrepresentation and misinterpretation of facts. It is really a pity that the 18th century European trader on the coast formed his view of the men around him and the 19th century missionary and administrators went out with a fairly fixed idea of what they would find and in most cases found them that way. Some of the writings did not let the data speak for themselves but the collectors rather forced them into preconceived scheme. The presupposition, however, difficult to avoid, should not have been pressed too far. The present writer had elsewhere critically analysed the pitfalls and strength of the genre of literature of the first two centuries of European contacts with Africa. It is sufficient to note that the class of literature and reports which formed the basic source of studying African religion and culture was:

> *derived from the same common source of human purposefulness that nourished the Mid-Victorian evangelical reforms, systematic thinkers and indeed captains of industry... they were not alone in this regard and to some extent, reflected in their writings if not in their perceptions the ... age distinctly conscious of its own civilization, particularly Burton's account being sullied for the present generation by blatant displays of pure prejudice.*[31]

The use of Comparative Method in Social Science is not entirely new or bad but if it is used primarily as a means to show the manifestly advanced position of the West, it is unfair, unscientific and prejudicial. With this preconception, it is unlikely that a reliable study of other people's culture and life-style could be embarked upon. Even when the intellectuals in the West had abandoned pride of race, pride of culture persisted in certain quarters. At the close of the 19th century, Mary H. Kingsley discredited the false views of Africa given by *stray travellers, missionaries and other colonial government officials who for their own aggrandisement exaggerated the difficulties and dangers with which they had to deal.*[32] She did not uphold everything African as all right but distinctly observed that a genuine attempt should be made to present valid and undistorted picture of the situation. Neither the missionaries nor the other European writers on Africa wrote books, according to Mary Kingsley, at the initial period of contact with a balanced and objective view of the situation. Although many cultural practices were not good enough to be accepted in modern times as standard norms of behaviour and life, it is obvious that many early visitors to Africa did not present good image of the continent. The nationalists, on the other hand, over reacted by trying to *glorify every aspect of the culture as valid and edifying*. Their attempt to defend Africa made them ignore obvious and glaring deficiencies in the traditional religious system, which provided explanatory category for the cosmology and world-view. This had in a subtle way constituted a clog in the wheel of development. The role of this religion will engage our attention in the second part of this book.

NOTES

1. J.D. Hargreaves (ed.0   *France and West Africa*. London: Macmillian & Co. 1969, p. 34

2. John Barbot   A Description of the Coasts of North and South Guinea(1732) in *A collection of Voyages and Travels, Vol. V.* (London, Meppicurs Churchill, MDCC, printed for Henry Lintot and John Osborn, 1746, p. 10

3. A.F..C Rider   *Materials for the study of African History in Portuguese Archives* London, University of London Press, 1965, pp. 1 - 3

    JH. Parry.   *Europe and a Wider World 1415 - 1715*. London, Hutchinson University Library, 1949, Reissued, 1960, pp 29 - 36

4. T. Hodgkins   *Nigerian Perspectives*, London O.U.P, 1975, p. 9

5. S. Hamdun & N. King   *Ibn Batutta in Black Africa* London: Rex Collins, 1975, p. 51

6. B. Davidson   *Black Mother*. London: Longmans & Co. 1961, p. 100

7. J. Barbot   ibid., p. 10

8.   T. Canot   *Memories of a Trader*(set down by Blantz Mayer and edited by W. Lawerence.(London: George Newness Ltd) n.d. pp. 54- 55

     B. Shaw (Lady Lugard)   *A Tropical Dependency.* London: Nesbit and Co. 1906, p. 339

9.   H. H. Roth   *Great Benin: Its Customs, Art and Horrors.* Halifax: F. Kings & Sons 1902, p. 1-2

10. H.H. Roth   ibid, p. 49ff

11. J. Barbot   Op. cit. p 352

12. J. Barbot   op. cit. p 34

13. R. Halkluyth   *Principal Navigations* Vol. 2. (1599 edition_, pt. 2, p. 19

14. U.R. Onunwa   The Study of West African Religions in Time Perspective. (Unpublished Ph. D. thesis, Univ of Nigeria, 1984, p. 46

15. W. Bosman   *A new account and accurate description of the Coast of Guinea* Utretch, 1705, Translated from Dutch and reprinted, 1907, p. 454

16. E.B. Idowu   African Traditional Religion: A Definition. London: SCM, Press 1973, pp 108 - 138

17. T. Hodgkins   Op. cit. p. 14

18. W. Hinschberg   *Monumenta Ethnographica* BD 1. (Schwarx- Africa, Gratz / Austria,) 1962, p. 51

19. R.A. Nisbet   *Social Change and History.* London , OUP, 1969, P. 139

20. C. White   *Accounts of the regular graduation of Man.* (London: 1799,) p. 1 and passim

21. C. de Brosses   *Cult of the fetish gods,* 1760. Reissued as Cults of the fetish gods or Parcels of Ancient Egypt's Religion and Actual Religion in Nigeria. Paris: 1960, p. 8

22. P.D. Curtin   *The Image of Africa: British Ideas and Actions of Empire 1780 - 1850.* Wisconsin: The University Press, 1964, p. 3

23. R.F. Burton   *A Mission to Gelele- King of Dahomey. Vol. 11,* 2nd Edition, London: Tinsley Brothers, 1864 p, 199

R. West   *Back to Africa: A History of Sierra Leone and Liberia.* London: Jonathan Cape, 1970, pp.188 - 190

24. R. I. Rotberg (ed.)   *Africa and Its Explorers, Motives, Methods and Impact.* (Cambridge Mass, 1970, p. 55 ff

    J. E. Harris(ed)   *Africa and Africans as seen by Classical Writers.* (Washington: DC., Howard University Press, 1977, passim

25. E.W. Smith (ed)   *African Ideas of God* London: Edinburgh House, 1951, p. 1

26. P.D. Curtin   Scientific Racism and the British Theory of Empire. Journal of Historical Association of Nigeria. Vol. 1, no. 2 (1960), p. 48

27. J.F. Schon & S.A. Crowther, Niger Expeditions: Journal of J.F. Schon and Mr. S.A. Crowther. London, Hatchard & Sons, 1842 , p. 50

28. P. Verger   The Yoruba High God: A Review of Source. *ODU*, 2,2, Jan. 1966, p. 23

29. M. Yu Funkel   Edward Blyden and the concept of African Personality. *African Affairs*, Vol. 72, Nos. 292 1974, p. 227

    H.R. Lynch   *Black Statesman: Selected Published Writings of E.W. Blyden.* London: Frank Cass & Co. 1971, p. xi ff.

    P. Esedebe   Wilmot Blyden 1832 - 1912 as a Pan-African Theorist. *Sierra Leone Studies* July 1969 pp 14 ff

    E. Holden   *Blyden of Liberia: An account of the Life and Labours of E.W. Blyden as recorded in Letters and Print.* (N.Y. Vantage Press, 1966), p. 111 ff

30. E.W. Blyden   *African Life and Customs.* London: 1908, p. xxxvii of the introduction

31. R.I. Rotberg   Op. cit., p. 5 –

32. M.H. Kingsley   *West African Studies.* London: 1899, 3rd Edition, Frank Cass & Co. 1964, See Introduction to the 2nd Edition, opposite the frontispiece.

CHAPTER THREE
Principal Elements in African Traditional Religion and Culture

In this chapter, we shall try to clarify some ambiguities surrounding the different sections in which the principal elements of African religion and culture are grouped. It will take a descriptive approach in the classification of the phenomena which form principal components of the religious and cultural system. We do not intend to go into deep analysis of the elements we have identified as Principal Components of the religious system. The votaries of the faith may not be aware of this classification, which takes a very streamlined and academic format. All the same, it does not seem strange to them as this is gleaned from what the typical African traditionalists believe in.

The aim of the chapter, therefore, is to delineate all that form the corpus of belief and practice, which have affected growth and human development in the universe from prehistoric times. The religious factor gives the spiritual impetus and moral basis for living. Besides, the chapter will help to clear the doubts in the minds of those who have for long been made to believe that African Traditional Religion is no religion at all. The elements herein described show that the indigenous traditional Africans perceive them as integral parts of a system they cherish and value. The argument whether African Religion is a religion or not is an overlaboured issue and is beyond the primary concern of this study.

The religion has from prehistoric times offered several generations of its votaries a perception of the Divine. Some basic practices and features and other peculiar principles of the religion are not discussed here because many indigenous and western scholars had covered such areas in their work and there is spate of literature, which now exist in the discipline since the 1950's. The Principal Elements constitute the core belief systems, which determine the rituals and other ethical behaviours. Consequently, they form the corpus of belief and influence as well as determine people's outlook and actions. Some scholars prefer to describe the religion in the plural- thus African Religions- because each ethnic group in Africa has its form of traditional religion with so many different and peculiar rituals that there hardly can be a centre of orthodoxy in what we describe as African Traditional Religion and Culture. People who hold this view believe that what Africans have is *African Traditional Religions and Cultures.*

On the other hand, there is a School of Thought, which believes that in spite of obvious differences in language, and rituals in different parts of Africa, the structure is basically the same. Different denominations or sects in some Missionary Religions do not necessarily make them different *Christianities,* or Islams. Whether it is African Religion and Culture or African Religions and Cultures, we shall take it to mean in this study as one homogenous religious and cultural system indigenous to African groups that profess it as faith. A five structural system is common to all forms of the religion found in the African sub-Sahara. The five-structural system is made up of:

Belief of the Supreme Deity
Belief in the Deities
Belief in Spirits
Belief in Ancestors
Belief in and practice of magic and medicines/charms.

3.1   Belief in the Supreme Being

African belief in the Supreme Being (God), in whatever local name they may address him- is a commonplace phenomenon in many communities. Unfortunately, this fact has been made a controversial issue by writers and interpreters of the faith of the Africans. Although some accorded African Traditional Religion the status of religion per se, they denied it the usual and important feature – that of belief in the Supreme Being. Every African society, known to the present writer, has got its own specific name for the Supreme Deity. The names so far examined are indigenous to those who use them. Some of the names are descriptive of some characteristics of God most conspicuous in the very community it is used. All the same, no African seems ignorant of the name his local community calls the Supreme God.

Sequel to the denial of belief in the Supreme God is worship of him in the entire African world. It had been the stand of many scholars that there is no Direct Cult of the Supreme Being in Africa. It has not been a problem of the votaries of the religion even though many of them could not explain why the situation exists. The ordinary votary of the religion in the rural communities usually expressed their experience of God as a Deity of three-fold revelations - *General Revelation, Conscience and History*! It is still doubtful if Africans know such a Supreme Being, the extent they carry out Direct Worship of him does not justify their claim. What is the relationship between such God and the rest of the creation in African myths and cosmology? In other words, to what extent is God present in human affairs? Is he a withdrawn God – the *Deus Otiosus* or *Deus Remotus* which some the early European writers branded him? At what time in human history did Africans come to acknowledge the Supreme God or become aware of his presence in the universe? These and many other questions have bothered scholars of African Traditional Religion and Culture as well as many cultural anthropologists. They sound too abstract and hypothetical to the African votaries of the religion who do not see their faith in purely cognitive way. To them, God is a practical Reality rather than a cognitive phenomenon.

In the recent past, two outstanding Africans had given prominence to the study of the belief in the Supreme Being as a long established fact in African traditional religious experience and expression.[1] John Mbiti did a follow up work on the one W. Abraham and Bolaji Idowu did in the 1950s on the Supreme Being.[2] The two scholars were not necessarily being nationalistic in their presentation of African belief and worship of the Supreme Being. They rather presented the facts as objectively as they knew them from the experience of their contact with the votaries of the religion.

Prior to the works of Abraham and Idowu, E.G. Parrinder, who closely followed Edwin Smith's methodology had by 1949 concluded that belief in the Supreme God was a central feature of African Traditional Religion. His work, which came out in the early 1950s, was the first comprehensive and systematic attempt by a conscientious scholar to get at the root of African belief in the

Supreme Being.[3] It must be acknowledged that Parrinder's extensive work in West Africa was instrumental to the opening of the study of African Traditional Religion as an academic discipline at the University College of Ibadan, Nigeria in 1948. The university was a college of the University of London built in the tradition of British University system in the colonies. Following the pioneering work of Parrinder at the University of Ibadan, many indigenous Africans have explored the meaning and relevance of the belief in the Supreme Being in some African societies. For instance, Emefie Ikenga-Metuh was so puzzled by the controversy that beclouded the belief in the Supreme Being by votaries of African Traditional Religion that he decided to explore the relationship between God and Man in Africa. He used the data from the Igbo of Nigeria to present a systematic view of the relationship, as he understood it from the people's way of life and thought. According to him, it is not a case of intellectual assent but a commitment, which is fully demonstrated in practical ways of life.[4]

Many scholars of African Traditional Religion and Culture have documented what they described as evidences they collected from votaries of the traditional religion to validate the claims that people believe in and worship the Supreme Being. These are without prejudice to the claims of earlier writers to the contrary. Some of the evidences include names of God collected from different ethnic groups, proverbs, myths, riddles, pithy sayings, cosmological views, oaths, curses, blessings, ejaculatory prayers and exclamations and finally the structure of African societies.

The Akans of Ghana in West Africa showed signs of their belief in God very clearly in their worship. Sir E.B. Ellis notices the signs and concluded that such clear belief found among the Akans might have been borrowed from their contact with the Europeans several centuries back. This was an untenable conclusion. The Akans did not have religious contacts with the pre-Missionary Europeans who came to West Africa. They came for commercial purposes and did not involve themselves in religious discourse with native Akans as to influence their religious world-view. Besides, the Akans call their Supreme Being, *Nyan Kopon*. Captain R.S. Rattray who came out much later than Ellis discovered that Akans as well as the Ashanti of the same Ghana, had a very ancient belief in Nyan Kopon, which was so established and remotely dated to the people's way of life prior to their contacts with either European Christian Missionaries or

Muslim traders. To Rattray, the belief was so old that it was indigenous to the Akans and the Ashanti as well. There is enough evidence to show that when anyone speaks about the Supreme Deity, the one is clearly understood by others. Rattray was able to discover that the Ashanti could speak about the Supreme Being and other minor deities without confusing one with the other. For instance, praise names, which the Akans give to God, reflect their existential experience. They have two names for God- the Supreme Being- *Nyan Kopon* or *Onyame*. They also call God other names like:

Bore- Bore	Creator
Amosu	Giver of Rain
Amovia	Giver of Sunshine
Pan Yin	Elder
Nana	Grand Father

Often, God is addressed as **Onyan Kopon Kwame**- the Great One of Saturday because he is worshipped on Saturday as his Sacred Day. This is where the Hebrew Judaism came close to the traditional African religious experience and practice. This close resemblance is still difficult to explain as Jews did not go out to evangelise the Akans and no Adventists came to the community till after several years when Missionaries had established Christian churches that worshipped God on Sundays. So the idea of worship of the Supreme Being on a Saturday, similar to the Jewish tradition, is quite indigenous to the Akans.

Many other Africans in the East, Central and South-African regional zones have their own peculiar experiences and understanding of the Supreme God. They may not understand the names or terms, which other groups used for the Supreme Deity but certainly, they were not ignorant of God within the context of their environment, experience and exposure.

Some of the names used for God are quite difficult to translate into other languages, as they are difficult to understand too. The illiterate adherents were unable to explain the meanings of the names properly to early European visitors and missionaries. That created a gap in communication and understanding. The controversy, which began in the early 1930s over the clear concept of the Supreme Being in Africa by indigenous Africans, was probably intended to justify the need for the missionary presence in the continent. Since the Africans had no knowledge of the Supreme Being and had no religion of their own, they were in urgent need of mission evangelisation and conversion to the knowledge and belief in the only one and Supreme God of the Christians. Those who believed that Africans had an idea of God (but nonetheless vague and unclear) were not sure when a clearer view came about. The speculation was that this took place probably around the time after Western contact with European Christian or Arab Muslim traders or explorers. This has been the problem of speculators and intellectual theorists. For the votaries such exercise was futile and irrelevant.

It might be likely that a clear concept of God was not a matter of one day's experience in Africa. It probably might have taken a long period of time as the religion and culture of the people developed and progressed. A few individuals and communities might have got the idea much earlier than others and from them it spread far and wide as people came into contact with others. A number of factors might have come into play for this – including extension of scale and shades, contacts with people of other races and culture and progressive revelation. It is still not acceptable to the votaries of African Traditional Religion that their belief in God was borrowed. It happened during the period of their contact with Christian Missionaries and Muslim traders and visitors. Culture contact affects people in two dimensions- *positive and negative*. The Hebrews, for instance, who claim the exclusive ownership of Yahweh as the God of their fathers, did not have a clear view of him till after several centuries of contact with him. Many generations after Abraham did not ask for the Special Name of the God of their fathers who had dealt so lovingly with them. Abraham who was described as a close friend of God did not give us the name of this friend of his who had been very generous to him. It was Moses who fearlessly demanded to know the name of the God of his fathers who appeared to him in the wilderness. This is the significance of the encounter at the Burning Bush (Exodus 3).

It was then that the name *YAHWEH*- which is a Hebrew gerund or verbal noun was disclosed to him. The name has undergone many changes and if it is a verbal noun as the Hebrew grammar suggests, it is impossible to be the real Divine Name of the God who had dealt very close with Abraham, Isaac and Jacob. In a similar way, that could the experience in many African communities where people had known and worshipped the Supreme Being in their own way for many generations long before contacts with European Christian Missionaries or Arab Muslim traders was made. It would be difficult to state that a very clearly streamlined belief and worship of the Supreme Being was there all the time. It might have taken a gradual process before the people got to a stage when they got a clearer grasp of what they believed in and worshipped.

Besides, one obvious fact that should be taken seriously in this case is the social behaviour prevalent in some African communities. For those who have come into close contact with Africans in the field, their idea of respect in many cases does not allow a younger person to address an elder by the elder's first name or personal names. He could use a nickname that shows respect and honour. The younger could also use the elder's title by which the elder is known in the community. In master/servant relationship, the same thing happens. So honorific titles and names have in most cases replaced people's real names. For instance, many Africans did not address their colonial administrators and Lieutenant Governors by their first names. They rather used official or professional titles of the officer concerned. Children and younger siblings do not address their parents and other senior members of their families by their first names. If this practice is taken back a little further, it might be one of the reasons Africans could not address the gods let alone the Supreme Deity by their real names.

On the other hand, we must not play down the possibility of the influence of the contact with Christians and Muslims on African concepts of the Supreme God. The microcosmic world view traditional to Africans was given a macro perspective by the contact with Christians and Muslims. Yet the place and frequency of the use of the name of the Supreme God in African myths is so ontological that one will not doubt that Africans had known and worshipped this God from a distant past, if myths are still believed to have a seal of antiquity.[5]

In Christian theology, the idea of God as a Father was a later introduction by Jesus Christ. This notion brought Jesus into conflict with the Jewish Religious Leaders who had been brought up to see Yahweh as Lord. Abraham and the other Patriarchs did not know Yahweh as Father but Jesus taught his disciples who were Jews, to see God as their Father. Revelations of aspects of God cannot be static but progressive and a similar thing could have happened in African traditional concept and experience of God. Each generation probably improved on the legacy handed over to it by the preceding generation. Progressive revelation is therefore, a very likely process of explaining how clearer notion and belief as well as worship of the Supreme Deity developed in African religion and culture.

3.2   Belief in Divinities

African worldview and classification of deities in many societies recognise fundamentally two types of deities- the Supreme Being and the Subordinate deities. The Supreme Deity is one but has as many ministers as there are areas of life to look after in human society. That is why each community has many deities in its pantheon of gods. It is just like a king having many representatives or agents in different parts of his domain. It is probably because the divinities are many and feature prominently in daily activities and affairs of people's lives that some scholars misunderstood the place of the Supreme Being as central in African religious life.   This misunderstanding brought in the problem of *terminology*. Is the African religion a *Monotheism*, *Polytheism* or *Pantheism?* The question is still a problem to those who do not belong to the religion but for the honest practitioners of the faith, it is none of their problems.   The religion is a system of life in which the votaries have not engaged themselves in any form of intellectual discourse of its dogma or theology. No votary of the traditional religion discusses it as if it were like any other form of political or social affair.

The Africans do not confuse the divinities with the Supreme Being. They rather see the divinities as ministers and functionaries of the Supreme Being which also serve as his intermediaries. A close study of African social systems will throw more light on this structural arrangement of the pantheon. The structure of the traditional society makes the existence of the divinities a necessity in the *theocratic administrative system of the universe.* Some of the divinities are seen as *emanations of the Supreme Deity* who gave them autonomous existence and power to oversee certain aspects of life in community. In that case, their existence is only a function of the Supreme Being. They are not ends in themselves but a means to an end. Their divine spark is derived from the limitless power of the Supreme Deity. The divinities do not compare in power or purity with the Supreme Deity although they exercise some great influence in certain cases. For that reason, some people who often take them to be sole and final authority in some matters have mistaken many divinities to be great spiritual forces.

There are two types of divinities- Major Divinities and the Minor Divinities. The first include all the natural phenomena which exist in the universe, and by the nature, size and the area of sphere of their influence which they exercise, they are known as the Major ones to be respected and worshipped. Their cult is widespread and people offer them daily worship and offerings. The deities in this group are many including the Earth Goddess, some rivers, moon god, sun god, some big trees, hills, and some other big animals. The Minor Deities are small patron gods and goddesses found in many communities. They are local and more often than not, represent local gods that look after local aspects of life in a community. Some of them become the patron gods of some professions, e.g. god of iron, or god of hunting, etc. They are worshipped in some villages or clans where their influence is only noticed and observed. A clan deity may be seen as a Minor deity but might be seen and worshipped as a Major Deity of a particular clan or village that worships it. So, the term Minor and Major may not be easily streamlined in some cases.

The Major deities are not seen as patron deities of any clan or community. For instance, the Sun God, which is a major deity in many African societies, does not have its shrine in every community in Africa. It may be found in some places as a very highly developed cult but non-existent in many others. The existence of some deities is somehow determined by ecological factors. For instance people who live in coastal villages or communities usually have a Water Goddess as their patron deity. Those who live in forest areas have gods of the forests or woods, while those in hilly areas have goods of the hills or caves. Those who have agriculture as the mainstay of their economy usually have *Land or Earth deities* that protect the farmers and their crops. To some extent, one may say that African deities are *functional*. They are meant to serve the needs of those who worship them. They, the gods, reflect the daily experiences of the local people.

One other idea that circulates in many places is that some people regard some deities as the female consort of the Supreme Being. For instance, the *Earth Goddess* is regarded as a female deity, which acts like a Mother to every other deity. The family image or concept is thus occasionally used to explain the relationship between the Supreme Being and the major and minor deities. The transcendental nature of the Supreme Being makes the existence of both the major and minor deities a theocratic necessity for governance of the universe on his behalf. They, therefore, act as his *functionaries, deputies and ministers*. Al though these major and minor divinities act as means to an end and seen as functionaries of the Supreme Being, some people unconsciously end up worshipping them without difficulty. They thus trust that the Supreme Being will ultimately receive any form of offering or worship offered to the Minor Deity who would surely render accounts to the Supreme Being.

From the above analysis therefore, one can conclude that the notion of the existence of divinities which receive daily offerings or which have regular cult is well established in traditional religious system of many African peoples. The number of such deities varies- almost every department of human life and endeavour has got its own patron deity or Guardian Deity. African world is a religious universe in which all aspects of life are properly protected by Guardian patron deities. The subordinate status of the divinities is variously expressed in terms of *Creator/Creature*, or *Father/Son*, Master/*Servant*, or *Husband/Wife* relationship. E. E. Evans-Pritchard has elsewhere described the deities in African Traditional Religion, especially among the Nuer of Sudan, as the sons and creatures of God. According to him,

> *The spirits of the air are nevertheless being Spirit of God they are many but also one. God is manifested in and in a sense is each of them*[6]

Among the Yoruba of Nigeria, Orisha is a generic name for the deities who are believed to have emanated from the Supreme Being- Olodumare. The term Orisha is never applied to Olodumare- as if he is one of the deities. He is wholly other than any being. He is completely unique in himself. The deities are therefore seen as Olodumare's ministers- who look after the affairs of the universe and act as intermediaries between the Olodumare and the world of humans. The major divinities are no more than some attributes of Olodumare, although some deities are believed to have independent existence.[7]

There is need to take the idea of Major and Minor Divinities a little further. The two terms imply the scope of the area of the operation and authority of a particular deity. Some are known and worshipped throughout a region or within a clan where their cults are established. The population of the votaries may run in thousands or millions. Some occasional clients may come from distant places to ask for help at the shrine in moments of sickness, death or attack by enemies. Though a particular deity may be seen or worshipped in a region where it is regarded as a major deity, its cult may not be established in every part of the region. It is also with a deity that we classify as minor. Its cult is established within a micro area with a few people as its votaries. Some clan deities often stand as major deities of the clan but cannot be classified as major in the sense of national cult and worship. What we may describe as a major deity may not be seen as a special major deity of a clan or village that has its own patron deity. For instance, the Earth Goddess is seen as a major deity in all the five identifiable subculture areas of Igboland but there are some villages that do not worship the Goddess as their own personal Patron Deity.

The moon, sun and some rivers are deities that perform important functions as major deities in many African societies. Yet in some communities, they do not have direct Cult and people do not offer sacrifice to them. There is no nation-wide established cult of the Sun and Moon in any part of Africa found by the present writer throughout his period of field research. Yet they are classified as major deities in Africa. Some big rivers like the Niger, Benue, Zambezi, and Congo have some people who worship them or have shrines erected at their shores. Yet not all Africans worship them as their major deities. The idea of major and minor is still something that has not got a pan-African label.

The notion of a *Withdrawn God* who is distant from the human world is strange to Africans. Although the idea of God looms high in the minds of Africans, the approach to him is more or less ambivalent. Organised direct cult of the Supreme Being in terms of elaborate altars, priests, rituals, festivals and sacrifices is rare to find. That is why the deities, rather than the Supreme Being, seems to be the central focus of religious life. The worshippers make no image or effigy of the Supreme Being. The apparent absence of the Supreme Being in daily affairs of humans made Mircea Eliade conclude that an African cannot stand the immense transcendence and abstract nature of the Supreme Being and has therefore, substituted him with other divine forms which he can manipulate to meet his daily and urgent needs.[8] That is not the true situation if Mircea Eliade understands the structure of many African societies where it is not proper for a junior or a subject to appear before his monarch every minute with problems and complaints. The African Society is monarchical in many ways and places and as such, the middlemen and intermediaries have prominent roles to play. So the presence and existence of the divinities as mid-way between the Supreme Being and humans is a theological as well as socio-political necessity. So the substitution theory, which Eliade seems to imply, does not mean absence of belief in or worship of the Supreme Being entirely. It rather tries to emphasize belief in the deities who act as *ministers and functionaries* of the Supreme Being. However, it must be stated that Eliade's use of the term *abstract*, is not true of the people's view of God. He is not an *abstract concept* in the thought of the traditional religion and culture in Africa.

The divinities are believed to be in charge of the day-to-day affairs of humans in the universe because of the cosmological ideas of the people who feel that it is not courteous to approach their King directly or bother him with daily problems of life, which his *junior ministers* could effectively solve. It is only when they fail or refuse to carry out the duty that a direct appeal to the Supreme Being becomes inevitable. This cosmological view must be understood in relation to African *concept of middleman* in transaction of ordinary business in human life. The middleman is important, but if he fails to carry out his own responsibility to the satisfaction of his client, a direct contact with the boss becomes inevitable. Prayers and sacrifices are constantly offered through the divinities for onward transmission to the Supreme Deity who is the *Ultimate Recipient* of all the offerings and petitions It is important that if the middlemen (divinities) are ignored or offended, they might quickly revenge by causing some misfortunes, premature death, disorder, epidemics or any other form of harm. They might even block the client's way to the Supreme Being. So one must try to be at peace with the deities through prayers, offerings, and moral living. Whenever misfortune strikes, an oracle is consulted. The diviner who is often regarded as an expert in peering into the spirit world diagnoses the causes of the problem with the use of his instrument, and prescribes the solution.

Votaries of Traditional Religion fear most of the popular deities especially those whose sphere of influence is widely spread. What makes some of them very formidable and terrifying is the fact that people believe whenever they (the divinities) strike or punish any culprit for an act of transgression, they give unmistakable signs that they have really struck. It is believed that anyone who swore to false oaths at the shrine of a powerful deity might suffer from swollen stomach or limbs or of any other despicable disease like leprosy, dropsy and oedema. People particularly fear the *god of thunder* whom they regard as the agent of the Supreme Being that detects any hidden crime committed anywhere in the universe.

In addition to some natural phenomena that are *deified*, there are many dangerous and powerful animals that are regarded as manifestations of the power of the Supreme Deity. Incidentally, such animals like the lion, elephant, python and cobra, crocodile or tiger are regarded as divinities in some communities. Some of the totems have long stories of sacred significance in the lives of some people in the communities behind their *deification* in the past. Some geographical features like caves, big hills, forests, volcanoes that inspire awe had been associated with stories of being locations of divine presence or epiphany. People had been made to believe that such locations might have been the dwelling place of the deities some time in the distant past. So sacred groves with some long mythical or legendary stories behind them are known to be locations of sacred importance. There is no confusion in the minds of the votaries as to where to draw the line between the Supreme Being and other spirit beings in the universe.

3.3   Belief in Spirits

Third in the order of hierarchy of the African pantheons are the Spirits. African beliefs became so prominent in the assessment of the early foreign writers that they described the whole African Religious system as *Animism*. The word is derived from the Latin word, **anima,** meaning **spirit.** The traditional African religious worshippers believe that there is spirit in every *inanimate* and *animate* objects. In other words, there is spirit in every thing- living and non-living. Although the whole religion and its cultural system could be said to be concerned with both *spirit* and *matter*, there is a way in which the idea of *spirit* pervades everywhere. The spirit could be good or evil, beneficial or harmful. The spirits inhabit any being or any object on permanent or temporary basis. Some of them even inhabit human bodies and if they are the evil or bad spirits, any person who harbours them might behave abnormally and often commit criminal acts that would prove harmful to both the person and the other members of the community in general. Such a person might die prematurely in some cases. Some spirits dwell in tress, rocks, and bush or in the atmosphere. They are invisible but their actions are visible. People also experience them and tell how those actions affect them. Some people have tried to explain the existence of spirits as *abstractions* or *emanations* of the Supreme Being or a *refraction* of the Divine which grows into separate and independent being. In other words, humans have used the concept of the spirit as a *category* to explain experiences in the universe.

The purpose of the existence of the spirit in the universe is not yet clear. Some priests of the traditional religion who tried to explain this to the present writer stated that they are *divine agents* that can be employed by humans to aid them in their daily struggles and undertakings. Unfortunately, some spirits impede human progress instead of helping human development. They are numerous in the universe. Our task in this case is to critically examine the influence of this belief on the life of those who hold it. This demands the study of African world-view and the beings that occupy it. This ontological study may not be given an in dept analysis here but a cursory look at it might throw some light on the second part of this work.

The *tutelary spirits that pervade the universe* affect humans in various ways. The prominent ones among them include the fairies, apparitions and the ubiquitous malevolent spirit called the *devil* or *evil spirit*. Many African peoples have specific names for the Devil in their own local languages. Incidentally, the devil is often seen as an enemy of the Supreme Being and goes about to haunt and molest people. In some cases, the role of the devil is *ambivalent*. On the one hand, it acts as the agent of the Supreme Being to punish a culprit and on the other hand, it enhances the opportunities of a good man to achieve a particular goal in life. This view is typical of the Yoruba of Nigeria who believe that the evil spirit- *Eshu-* is the enemy of God – *Olodumare-* on certain occasions and on some others serves as his powerful and useful agent that carries out his commands and goes on errands for the Supreme God. This belief has made the Yoruba treat Eshu as an unpredictable spirit that must be feared and often wooed.

There is a distortion of the concept of the Evil Spirit in the work of some earlier writers who tried to find an equivalent Christian or Biblical view in African belief system. Their attempt has led to the falsification of the theology of the belief in Spirits in Africa. The Lugbaraa of Uganda, for instance, have a strong belief in spirits. The traditional Acholi and Lango concept of the Jok as spirits is quite different from what foreign interpreters of the Ugandan traditional religion made it. To the traditional votaries of the faith, the concept of the Jok among the Acholi and Lango people is one of the neutral, all pervading forces which inherently are neither good nor evil. However, some wicked men and women especially sorcerers can harness the power of Jok for selfish ends by using it to harm their rivals and enemies. The medicine men can use the power of Jok in public ceremonies for the good of the entire community. For instance, in the dry season, they can make rain for farmers through the power of the Jok. They use the power of Jok to help their own people achieve their genuine and good desires in life especially barren women in need of children. Many farmers, traders and sick people have been helped to achieve good success through the power of Jok.

The African Inland Mission (A.I.M.) which evangelised some parts of Uganda and translated the Bible into local languages identified the Jok with the Biblical Satan that deceived Adam and Eve and tempted Job too. The translators used the name of the lesser spirit in Acholi called *Lubango* to designate the Supreme God, an error that has persisted in Uganda for some time now. This is similar to what happened in some other African societies where the missionaries translated the Bible into the vernacular. The error was not intentional but has distorted the traditional concepts of the people. The Christian missionaries wanted to find a local equivalent concept of evil that would fall in line with either Christian or Western view. We have seen in recent times that it is not easy to provide a   Biblical equivalent to the African concept of the evil spirit without distorting the traditional viewpoints. It may be pertinent to mention Le Roy's earlier classification at this point. According to him,

> *although, evil spirit is regarded as sort of diffused power that can be controlled to a certain extent, yet there does not seem to be in the mind of Blacks, a Supreme power of Evil at strife with Supreme Power of Good. Such systematic dualism that some have thought to find in Africa does not exist there. It is a product of preconceived ideas that cannot stand simple and sincere observations of facts. The prince of evil or chief of hell is lacking in the vocabulary of the Bantus and of the Africans generally.*[9]

Le Roy's ideas are not entirely correct when seen within the context of the philosophy of *inseparable dualism* that has characterised African life and thought for a long time. The view upholds the existence of things in direct opposite to the other or in complementary form e.g.

Black	and	White
Long	and	Short
Male	and	Female
Life	and	Death
Dry	and	Wet
Good	and	Bad
Day	and	Night.

Each is a direct opposite of the other and in a way complements it. Life in many African societies goes in such inseparable pairs and rhythm. It is a rhythm that occurs naturally.

There is a divided opinion on this view. Some people do not have any spirits that is ontologically evil because according to them, any spirits has the potential to do both good and evil. Others believe that there are spirits that are *naturally* evil in their being and actions. Those who hold the first view state that so-called evils spirits were the *disincarnate human spirits* that probably absorbed the power of non-human spirits. Because they did not *re-incarnate* or were prohibited from doing so into the human world of time and space, they act in groups of anonymous spirits and attack individuals, families or whole community. They go in groups and act in concert and usually attack their victims with formidable force. They are the spirit of the dead who did not actually receive befitting funeral rites and in frustration and anger, decided to act within the caucus of *Age Grade System or Peer Group*. Some are called the forest *monsters or little people*. Such spirits are better exemplified by the Akans Spirits called *Sassbosam and Mmoatia*.[10]

Among the Igbo of Nigeria, evil spirits are basically apparitions of the dead and are classified into three groups. They are the:

Umu- aro	evil spirits of the dead children
Ogbonuke	evil spirits of dead young people
Akalogoli	evil spirits of adults who died childless and wicked

None of these spirits according to Igbo ritual laws was placated with befitting funeral rites. The denial of adequate funeral and burial rites could make the spirits of a dead person restless in the Spirit World- a reason for which it goes about the universe harassing human beings who are living in the Human World. The question again, is at what point in time, did these un-placated spirits become evil- at creation or as a result of denial of good and befitting funeral rites? If the Supreme Deity is the creator of all things, did he create these spirits evil from the beginning?

Among the Umu-aro spirits, there is another micro-group of spirits, which the Igbo call *Ogbanje*. The Yoruba of Nigeria call it *Abiku*. Many other ethnic nationalities in Africa have their own specific names for this type of malevolent and capricious spirit where it exists. Often, it may be an empirical way to explain otherwise difficult phenomena in human society. The sufferings of women who lose their babies in infancy have been attributed to the activities of this notorious evil spirit. People believe that this evil spirit is made up of a collection of children who died prematurely and thereby constitute themselves *into born-to die* in any child they entered or wanted to enlist in their group in the Spirit World. The belief is beyond any empirical analysis as it is within the realm of faith of the votaries of the traditional religion and culture. When the group of Ogbanje spirits enter any child conceived in the womb, it is believed that they sign a pact and enter into a covenant with that unborn baby in the womb. The secret covenant is beyond the empirical knowledge of the living. Such a baby which enters into a secret covenant and pact with its peers in the spirit world, is given a mandatory period of time to live and sojourn on earth after which it returns to join its peers in the spirit world. This would thus leave the bereaved mother in distress. This syndrome might repeat a number of times to the distress of the woman. J. O. Lucas describes the Ogbanje (Born-to-die) spirit in children in a graphic and lucid way:

> a confraternity of spirits who visit the world in incarnate form for short periods, the length of each being pre-arranged... The Spirits are born into babies who die in infancy to boyhood.[11]

The fear of the misfortune of Born-to-die syndrome is gradually being removed from the minds of many mothers in Africa. This mind-set is gradually changing through education, modern medicine and Christian enlightenment. Previously, many women were tormented through continuous and serial loss of their babies in infancy. The problem of Infant mortality was rife in many developing African nations due to a number of endemic problems of poor hygiene, poor paediatric care, poor medical care and poor food. The Ogbanje born-to die syndrome was a very clever and meaningful traditional explanation to the persistent problem faced by the society. The gradual removal of this problem of infant mortality is primarily due to improved health care delivery system and mother craft. The modern medical care through the services of many national and international Humanitarian Agencies like the United Nations Children's Emergency Fund (U.N.I.C.E.F), the World Health Organisation (W.H.O.), Save the Children's Fund (S.C.F.), among others, have improved the life expectancy of both mother and child. For instance, the deadly sickle cell that is genetically endemic among the Black Race is being monitored and controlled in many developing countries of the world. The introduction of neonatal care in some paediatric units in many hospitals has also added impetus to the human fight against killer diseases and particularly infant mortality. Probably, the Born-to – die syndrome was the meaningful explanation to the persistent infant mortality in many primary African societies. The disappearance is steady and progressive.

3.4   Belief in Ancestors

The Cult of Ancestors is a well-established system in many African societies. It is still popular in many communities because of the nature of African cosmology and social system. The importance of this cult is probably due to the strong family attachment existing in Africa. Its highly exalted position in the religio-cultural system was grossly misunderstood and misinterpreted by the early writers and anthropologists. The zeal and commitment to the Cult was so magnified out of proportion in African world-view that the early writers daubed the entire religious system *Ancestor- Worship*. What the Cult of Ancestors underlies, according to some learned traditional priests of African Religion, is the belief that death does not terminate the strong filial attachment in Africa. Death looms high in the traditional cosmology and every one fears it as a dangerous enemy. Yet this enemy does not terminate the links between loved ones. The departure of the elders to the Spirit World has only extended their life beyond this visible world of time and space. Thus, the cult of ancestors is strong evidence that Africans believe in *life after death or life after life*. It is a type of life which only those who were good in this physical world and lived transparently honest life continue to enjoy even after death. While enjoying this life, those elders would continue to undergo *series of re-incarnation* endlessly. They would certainly continue to enjoy the fellowship of the good ones who had gone before them and received the filial obedience from those still alive on earth. It is believed that in the life beyond the grave, those who led wicked life on earth would live in torment or in a state of denial of happiness. They are eternally plunged into *a place of no abode* or might return to the human world in form of harmful spirits or lower creatures to torment the living. (See section iii above on belief in spirits). This is the African expression of the Biblical concept of *Heaven and Hell*. The belief in the Cult of the Ancestors could be properly understood as an equivalent to the belief in the Communion of the Saints in Christian Theology.

John Mbiti, has suggested the term, *Living Dead*, to designate the ancestors who were once alive on earth but now dead and live in the Spirit World. They often return to the human world in reincarnation as babies into the families they once loved and lived in. It must be stated here that not all dead people are canonized as Ancestors or can be addressed as *Living Dead* elevated to the revered Cult of Ancestors. To be thus honoured demands the fulfilment of certain obvious conditions. These include:

Death at a ripe old age
Transparently honest life on earth
A viable descent group or lineage
Appropriate or befitting burial and funeral rites
Good death not by any despicable diseases like dropsy or leprosy.

The fulfilment of all the above five conditions may not be necessary in all African societies. For instance, an ethnic group in Tanzania does not believe in the concept of punishment by any one after death if the family members were able to forgive a dead man all his sins and misbehaviour committed while alive on earth. If they could declare that forgiveness at the graveyard during the interment, the dead would not suffer in the Spirit World.

Ancestors constitute a special category of spirits and occupy a special place in African world –view and traditional cults. The ancestral cult influences the lives of the votaries of the faith in such a way that every adult member of the society had his own shrine of the family ancestors and would be glad to be honoured like that after own death. There is a large collection of the effigy of all ancestors in a family or lineage and it acts as a form of family album or directory whenever they are displayed in the family gallery.

The ancestors are seen as spirits who have got an enhanced power and status. They could use their close relationships with the Supreme Being and the other deities to intercede on behalf of their living relatives and wards. With their clearer knowledge of the spirit world, as well as the human world, where they had lived before death, the ancestors constantly warn their living descendants and relatives of the dangers of leading bad lives here on earth. They not only direct them on how to win the favour of the divinities and the Supreme Being, but also plead on their half as their *Intercessors* and *Advocates* in the Spirit World. Hence Africans believe that *one whose father is active and powerful in the Spirit World would never have problems on earth*. Unconsciously, in many communities, the ancestors are elevated to the rank of *Deities*. Often some great deities are addressed as father great father, etc in prayers, probably they might be early ancestors who lived in long prehistoric times and had metamorphosed into the stage of deity. As members of families and clans where they had lived before becoming ancestors, the living dead are very concerned and interested in the welfare of the community and living members of each society. They are, therefore, regarded as the custodians of the traditional moral laws and customs on which the survival of the clan depends. Consequently, there is a constant offering of sacrifices to the ancestors- to appease them, to win their favour and support as a mark of filial obedience of minor to the elder in a society that recognises and respects old age. The ancestors are seen as close intercessors before God in every African society. The offerings may be seen as *Ancestor Worship* or *Ancestor Veneration*. Yet the terms have never been of any doctrinal problem to the honest votaries of the faith. The unsettled intellectual debate among scholars on the appropriate term to use, is still the problem of those outside the faith. The argument is now an over flogged issue and is no longer of any special interest to modern researchers. However, those still interested in the argument can refer to a number of works already published on it by other scholars.[12] Africans *worship* and *venerate* their ancestor. The practical approach to the spirit world through the ancestral cult is more important to the votaries of the faith than the terms which detached scholars use to describe a people's cherished acts of faith and rituals.

3.5   Belief in Magic (Practice of Medicine)

African traditional religion is full of *magical* practices. They look magic because they do not easily look logical to the uninitiated. Magic is not peculiar to African region but common in all world religions. It is in fact the feature of every religious system and has been described as the *elder brother of religion*. It was stated the primitive man resorted to religion when magic, which he had practised for a long time failed him. Early anthropologists described the *religion of the primitive man as magic*. The evolutionary trend in Western scholarship, which held the view that religion grew out of magic, has always described both magic and religion *as compatible bed mates*. It insists that there is little or no difference between the rituals performed by both systems. Both had the same generic beginning.

The underlying principle of magic is the belief in spirit pervasive forces, which can be harnessed for the benefits of humans on earth. Such forces can be both *productive* and *destructive*. Magical practices take the forms of charms, amulets, some sacrifices, sorcery and witchcraft. It is difficult to draw the line between magic and religion. They are interwoven and interrelated. The connotation *magico-religious,* had often appeared in works of some earlier writers on African cultural systems in a derogatory sense but a close study of the system shows that the term is not far from the truth. The essential difference between magic and religion is the objective expressed in the motto of magic-, which is, *let my will be done* and that of religion – *let thy will be done.* This motto has got a long-term spiritual implication in the practice of religion and magic in traditional African society and in fact in all primary societies. In religion, the worshipper commits things into the hand of the Divine who is the *Determiner and Destiny* of all whereas in magic, *my will be done,* emphasises man's ambitious and insatiable quest for power to bring all things under his control in order to satisfy his selfish needs and desires.

Traditional occultism deals with secrets of spiritual powers and how to use them to bring solution to human needs and problems. It involves the search for the hidden meaning of things and attempts to acquire and gain knowledge of events happening in this life in several places and around each person as well as inside him. Thus there is a fervent quest for *esoteric knowledge.* Divination, necromancy, vision, clairvoyance, among others, falls within this area of African Spirituality. The ability to harness the mystical forces in nature for good of man is a commendable exploration into Nature but it can be and has been used on many occasions to harm people.

There is a close relationship between *witchcraft* and *sorcery* in many African societies. The concern of this work is not to argue whether witchcraft exists in Africa or not. The rationale behind it is beyond the scope of this enquiry. It is obvious that Africans believe in it and practise it as an integral part of their religious system. A form of it is still practised in modern cities and in some African found Independent churches. If it is folly, it then falls with the folly of religious faith in general. If it is valid, then it could be understood as one of the tools, which Africans use to explore and explain the universe for the good of humans in it. It is, important to note that some forms of witchcraft are still practised in many industrialized Western countries. Human society has not completely got rid of it. Common to both witchcraft and sorcery is the belief that certain individuals have the power to harm fellow human beings by manipulating some supernatural forces. Some people use both terms interchangeably. However, they are two distinct phenomena. The present writer has fully explained the difference and similarity elsewhere.[13] E. E. Evans-Pritchard who did another work on witchcraft and sorcery among the Azande also analysed the differences between the two. According to him, the Azande distinguishes between witches and sorcerers and against both, they employ diviners, oracle and medicine men.

According to Azande taxonomy, a sorcerer achieves his evil ends by magic whereas a witch (in most cases) uses mystical powers of her personality to achieve the desired goal. A sorcerer casts spells and uses instruments and incantations but a witch does not. A sorcerer sends a message or messenger to cause harm on an enemy. Sorcerers often do their attack in their conscious state either by day or night but the witch does hers while in an unconscious state especially at night or day but asleep. It must be noted that women especially the very old and helpless ones, are often accused of being the perpetrators of evil through witchcraft. A few men are known to be members of the secret guild of witches. The destructive spirit of witchcraft can be despatched while a witch is asleep or in a trance. The idea of eating of the soul and sucking of the blood of a victim is a spiritual exercise and experience, which had tremendous physical effect on victims of attack of witchcraft. People believe that witches eat the soul and suck the blood of their victims. Some nocturnal birds and animals like the bat, owl and cat are associated with witches as objects which the witch can transform into in order to harm a victim. The witch could transform into any of the animals or birds through the process of metempsychosis and cause bodily and spiritual harm on an individual. The sorcerer may cast spell and cause a motor accident in a distant town and this could lead to the death of the targeted enemy. The ability of Africans to tap some natural forces in the universe to improve human conditions here on earth is understandably called *good* or *white magic*.

Some traditional men and women have been able to use herbs and roots of plants to cure diseases and protect people from untimely death. Furthermore, some have used similar objects including bizarre and weird ones, to cause harm on human society and people. Good magic may be used for the benefits of the entire community or for an individual person and his family. This can happen on occasions when rain is made during drought. A community can rejoice they invite some *rainmakers* to help them *manufacture rains* for farm work on a very hot day in dry season.

In many cases, the practice of *Black Magic* or *Evil Magic* has dominated the whole scenario and people have misused God's given ability for the destruction of humanity and society. This is seen as evil in African societies. Human and social developments have suffered huge set backs in many communities when fear of witchcraft dominates or suspicion of witchcraft and misuse of psychic and spiritual powers to harm progressive individual who could have contributed to the growth of the society prevail. Often, many mishaps in society or personal tragedies are explained in terms of witchcraft attack on persons.

Healing and protection of human lives from sudden and tragic deaths and misfortune through the use of herbs and traditional medicine can be seen as positive use of God's gifts to humanity. Many traditional healers, orthopaedic surgery practitioners and bonesetters and traditional midwives have contributed a lot to the health care delivery of the society. There is a very strong African belief in the use of traditional herbs for the cure of many ailments. This healing aspect of, though a special ministry on its own, can be seen as part of *Good Magic* or *White Magic*. Positive use of natural resources can enhance life expectancy and Africans believe that humans have the power and knowledge to tap God's given resources in the universe for the good of humanity.

The witch is *covenanted* into the cult by parents or senior siblings, who do such things, at times, without the consent of the minor. It is often done so early in one's life that many people have come to believe the notion that some *people are born witches*. It is this early initiation into the cult that makes one think that he is born with witchcraft genes. There are others who are initiated into the guild of witches in adult age and yet there are others who join because of peer pressures and the excitement of the wonders of the Spirit World.

The case of sorcery is in majority of cases a question of personal decision made by an individual to join a group that gives him joy or fun. A novice learns the art of manipulation of objects to produce desired results on a targeted individual or property. While sorcery is learnt skill and trade, witchcraft is normally a cult into which a person is initiated with or without the person's conscious volition. Many of those who were initiated young find out later of the long term destructive implications of their membership. Some of the young people who were initiated into the guild may not begin to manifest the *power* till late adolescence.

The five-structure bears out elements, which can be seen in a clearly spelt-out summary. These are, strong belief in:

i. The Supreme Being- his existence, worship, relationship with the world of man and the world of spirits

ii. Divinities- major and minor, human spirits mostly associated with the natural forces, minor divinities and their cults together with those of the other two.

iii. Spirits- tutelary spirits in the universe pervading all creatures

iv. Man- his creation, origin, destiny, marriage and other rites of passage, death, burial, hereafter, ancestral cults.

v. Mystical forces and powers- magic, witchcraft, sorcery, secret societies, religious personnel- priests, medicine men, prophets, diviners, clairvoyants, etc.

Conclusion

It is important to have a clear view of the structure of what Africans believe in a practise. It this very body of belief and practice that has affected, directed, and controlled their life-style, thought and action. More often than not, we may not fully appreciate the effects of some of the features we have outlined above on human development, progress and contribution to the world. Most of the above factors are no mere epi-phenomenon on society. They have direct or indirect effect on the events in society.

NOTES

1.   E. B. Idowu   *Olodumare: God in Yoruba Belief.* London: Longmans, (1962)

     cf. E. B. Idowu   *African Traditional Religion: A Definition.* London, SCM (1973)

2. J.S. Mbiti — *Concepts of God in Africa.* London SPCK, 1970, Reprint, (1993)

3. E.. W. Smith — *African Ideas of God.* Edinburgh House Press, Reprint (1961)

4. E.I. Metuh, — *God and Man in Africa.* London Geoff Chapman, 1981.

E.I. Metuh, — *Comparative Studies of African Traditional Religion.* Onitsha Nigeria: Imico Pub. 1987, pp 88, Reprint, 1997

5. U. Onunwa — *African Spirituality: An Anthology of Igbo Religious Myths.* Darmstadt, Germany, Thesen Verlag Wowincle, (1992). pp 1 – 10

6. E. E. Evans-Pritchard — *Nuer Religion.* Oxford, Clarendon Press, 1962. pp 51

7. Idowu, — *Olodumare,* ibid. p. 63

8. Mircea Eliade — *Patterns of Comparative Religion.* London: Sheed Ward, (1958). p 52

9. Alex Le. Roy — *The Religions of the Primitives.* N.Y. Negro University Press, 1969

10. K. O. Opoku — West African Traditional Religion. Accra Ghana, F.E. B. Int. Publishers, 1978, p. 2

11. J.O., Lucas — *Religion in West Africa and Ancient Egypt.* Reprint. Lagos, Nigeria, National Press, 1970. p. 168

12. E. G. Parrinder — *African Traditional Religion.* London: Longmans 1954. Reprint, 1976.

J.S. Mbiti — *African Religions and Philosophy.* London. Heinemann 1969.Reprint 1995 p. 85ff

E.I. Metuh — *Comparative Studies in African Religion.* Ibid. p. 156

Jomo Kenyatta — *Facing Mount Kenya.* London: Secker and Warbug, 1961, p. 263

13. U. Onunwa — Studies in Igbo Traditional Religion. Obosi Nigeria: Pacific Publishers, 1990, Reprint, 2004. Chap. 5

14. E. E. Evans-Pritchard — Witchcraft, Oracles and Magic: God Among the Azande. Oxford: Clarendon Press. 1937 p. 21

CHAPTER FOUR
Cultural Developments in Pre-colonial African Societies

(Selected Examples)

Introduction

A visit to any archive, museum or art gallery in Europe will display a vast array of ancient crafts, and artefacts of African origin. Traders or colonial officials who wanted to preserve some of the aesthetic objects they collected from their journeys took some of them out of Africa. Many of those objects were of immense value to the people who owned them and were of enormous ornamental values in those communities. Those materials among others are evidence of existing high technology and development of local crafts and culture in different parts of African in the distant past. There are also several forms of architectural designs, iron and metal casting, arts, stone and woodcarvings, beautifully decorated pottery, and bronze works. Some of the materials date far into the distant past in the communities where they were produced and used. In other words, many works of art on ivory, iron, copper, clay, bronze and stone existed in many ancient cities and centres of cultures in different African societies before their contact with European or Arab traders and visitors. Those who assess underdevelopments from its historical perspective state that it is a condition in which an exploited society is left by those who ravaged and looted its valuable property and wealth. Therefore, Dale Johnson has stated that *underdevelopment is a state which grew out of the relations between industrialised Western powers and their colonies.*[1] Invariably, colonisation was a factor of underdevelopment of Africa. Many African societies, had for instance, produced powerful weapons of war with which they resisted the attack from colonial soldiers. Some had also produced versatile agricultural implements with which they grew their food.

Some forms of writing were developed in different parts of Africa and in fact some regions developed scripts that lasted for some centuries before they became extinct. Some archaeologists have been able to do some excavations of sophisticated weapons and decorations used in some of parts of Africa, several centuries long before their contact with European and Arab traders and merchants. Some of the sites of those excavations were discovered to be graves of prominent leaders and rich local chieftains and kings. Others were sitting rooms and bedchambers of some prominent local leaders who ruled in the mini republics that existed. They were obviously manifestations of a type of standard of living among the rich in societies that were at the peak of their own development before impacted upon by several external invaders including Colonial administrators and traders. The disappearance of those ornaments and jewellery clearly point to a process of decay that was occasioned by a lot of other factors.

We shall validate our viewpoints with data collected from works of art that flourished in different parts of Africa in the distant past. They could be described as the legacies of *the Golden Age of Africa in the period of innocence* long before her contact with foreign traders, merchants, explorers and later colonial administrators. In spite of the glowing tribute which many African scholars pay to their ancestors' *noble and glorious past,* it is still difficult for one to imagine why so highly developed a civilisation and industrialisation could not continue to grow in the face of the onslaught of external agents of change and invading powers from the West.

4.1   Nigerian Arts and Sculptures

Preliminary Investigations

This was one of the greatest collections of human art that the present writer stumbled at while studying in the United Kingdom. Although he had heard so much of legendary artists and carvers and sculptures from that part of West Africa, it was his time in the British Universities that he came face to face with a huge collection of artefacts from there.

Many countries and zones in Africa had produced enormous artefacts and prominent works of art in stone, wood and iron at different periods of their history and development. The Congo Basin, Egypt and the Nile Region, Ethiopia and the West African Coasts have museums that are still full of beautiful works of art that are indigenous to the people. We shall pick a few examples from different parts of the continent to illustrate the level of cultural development, which flourished before the process of decline set in. Much of our knowledge of the pre-colonial African art is gleaned from archaeological excavations displayed in some of the museums and art galleries in Africa and Europe. The presence of some of those artefacts in Europe gives credence to the claims of the African nationalist writers that their culture was looted by early travellers and colonial administrators who helped themselves with the beautiful and ornamental carvings and works of art they could lay hands on during their sojourn in Africa. The history of artistic works of many countries is not a continuous one especially in places where wars, Trans-Atlantic and other international Slave Trades persisted for a long time. Much of the information gleaned from the works of art came from reconstruction of events. Its reliability is still questionable and of course no record can be bias-free .Yet there is no other way to extract information from the rich mines of knowledge embedded in the arts themselves. There are lots of gaps to be filled in the reconstruction of the history of the artefacts. Besides this weakness, it is important to note that such objects speak of a time when people were productive and creative in their thinking and construction.

The present writer was privileged to witness the *Exhibition of Nigerian Arts* at the Royal Academy of Arts in London. As a postgraduate research student who was collecting data for a doctoral thesis, he was privileged to attend the exhibition several times. The event was opened on Thursday, 28th October 1982 and lasted till January 1983. The opening ceremony was performed by Late Sir Edward Heath, one time Prime Minister of Great Britain. Prior to the exhibition, the delicately crowned head of the Oni, the King of the city of Ile-Ife, a city believed by the Yoruba of Nigeria to be the Cradle of human race, was displayed at every corner in London.[2] This symbol that was used as the Logo to advertise the exhibition was competing for attention of travellers at the London Underground with the advertisement for drinks and cigarettes. It was just to show how wide the publicity for the exhibition was for over a period of three months. When eventually the ceremony was opened to public on 30th October 1982, two days after its official opening, the archaeologist who saw some of the bronze casts, which were delicately wrought and attributed to Ile-Ife, thought that *the lost city of Atlantis has been discovered.* It must, however, be stated that the ancient city of Ile-Ife is still ruled by the Oni, who is regarded as a Sacred King and a progeny of Oduduwa, the god who created the ancient world according to Yoruba Myth of Creation. Frank Willet, a one-time professor of archaeology at the Department of Antiquities, University of Ife, Ile-Ife (now Obafemi Awolowo University, Ile-Ife), was by the time of the exhibition in 1982 the director of the Hunterian Museum in Glasgow, Scotland. He described the public reaction in the United Kingdom and Canada (where similar exhibition of Nigerian Art and Sculpture had taken place earlier) as exceptional. According to him, *it was the first time they had seen African Art of this type as distinct from modern sculpture. In the United States, there was a special factor in its appeal to the Black Communities. It broke all previous records for an art exhibition in the city and we sold more than five thousand catalogues.*[3] Frank Willet believed that the London Show of 1982-1983 would have wide appeal because there were Black Communities interested in African history as well as general public and those who follow the art closely. Some of the things displayed during the exhibition were new to a sculptor who had been collecting African art for a long time. Many of the objects exhibited were known to the archaeologists but not necessarily to people interested in African Art. It obviously dawned on many Africans that their ancestors were skilled people whose wonderful productions of art and culture were either destroyed or carried away. Unknown people carried the sources of wealth of those African ancestors away to foreign lands. The underdevelopment of their children and great grand children had been predicated on that misfortune. Their successors could have lived on the great legacies of their ancestors.

The Exhibition in London made the present writer explore more of the fate of the rich cultural environment and background that produced those wonderful works of art. Why the decline? What happened? These and other questions came up in the minds of many Africans who attended the exhibition and created the desire to probe deeper into African cultural history and production long before the period of contacts with European missionaries, traders, explorers, merchants and colonial officers. A few of the works of art found in many parts of Africa which date far back into such periods of history would be analysed here as models and paradigms of a form of technological development that flourished in the areas of culture, sculpture, pottery, carving and iron works. The highly sophisticated works of art depicted a class of advanced technology of its own in the distant past. They still challenge the ingenuity of the present generations of Africans in the area of technology, science, industrial development and education. Is the traditional African intelligence declining? It is not only in the area of arts and sculpture that people made progress in human development. Some outstanding feats were recorded in areas of local sports, traditional medicine, building technology, food production, etc. If the ancestors were able to produce the materials of such advanced level of development and skill that kept them alive in their own environment, why were those who succeeded them not able to keep the pace or improve on what they inherited? Why are the present generations of Africans not involved in inventions that can challenge the *Industrialized nations of the world*? It may be too simplistic to attribute all the causes to the invasion and conquering of Africa by the West through Slave Trade and later colonisation, but it would be too naïve to ignore the long term impact of those two weapons of dehumanisation and destruction of people's psyche, identity and self-esteem.

The challenge that the modern Africa faces now is how to recapture and restore the spirit and wisdom that produced that ancient and glorious technology. Restoration is not enough but to move on from that level to an advanced stage in contemporary world affairs. It is hoped although it may take some time, it is not completely impossible to adopt a mission strategy that can open new opportunities to development.

4.2   The Nok Culture

From the London Exhibition of 1982 – 1983, a wonderful observation was made. The challenge, which the exhibition threw to many Africans, was a renewed interest and quest for the discovery of many other useful cultural artefacts and their places of origin. It was known that there were many more African cultural materials that were hitherto hidden in different parts of the world under strict curators who do not want the original owners to know anything about them. It was discovered that more than two thousand years ago, there existed a form of civilisation that produced works of art unknown to any other people of the world. This form of art was called Terracotta. Modern historians, archaeologists, anthropologists and ethnologists have been struggling to locate the home base of this new cultural artefact. The *Terracotta* is still difficult to locate.

Brief History of the Terracotta

The present writer discovered that nothing similar to this work of art was known elsewhere in Africa let alone in the other parts of the world. No other part of the world had ever claimed it as a part of their cultural heritage. The *terracotta* are beautifully crafted perspective depiction of human as well as animal figures. The history is remotely associated with a group of tin miners who were working around the Jos Plateau in the Middle Belt Region of Northern Nigeria. In the past, tin mining in Nigeria was developed as one of the greatest industries in the country. It used to be one of the most important exports and foreign exchange earner for the country before the discovery of crude oil. When Nigeria became an independent and sovereign nation in 1960, tin was the most valuable mineral product from the Northern part of the country. The tin mining town of Jos attracted many European visitors and residents who settled there because of its cool and temperate climate that suited non-Africans who worked for the multinational companies that owned the Mining Industry and business. It was in the course of the mining activities that one of the miners came into contact with a strange discovery in the mines. When foreign experts and geologists, miners and archaeologists at the Mine, examined it, it was noticed to be a different material from the ordinary tin ore from the Mine.

The discovery of the NOK artistic figures was accidental. The archaeologists and geologists, using their carbon dating system, estimated the figures to have existed from between 500 BC and 200BC. This shows that there had been a form of civilisation and learning existing in this part of Africa in prehistoric times, even long before the emergence of many well-documented and known world philosophers and civilisations. What historians and archaeologists have not been able to ascertain is the origin of the NOK people who dwelt in the region where the Nok Terracotta figures were found. What happened to the original people who lived there previously? No one knows whether they migrated to any other part of the world. If they did, they could have established similar sculptures there or might have carried away some of the ones they erected at NOK. Besides, archaeologists could have made some discoveries of similar structures and figures in other parts of the world since the last 200 BC. But nothing similar to the NOK figures has been found anywhere in the world yet. Probably, the people died out and left their culture to lie dormant until the excavation at NOK during the tin mining business.

NOK is known to be earliest iron-smelting culture thus far discovered in Sub-Saharan Africa. Their sculptured Art's tradition depicted largely human and animal figures, the former in more or less stylistic form while the latter in a form of naturalistic pattern and designs. Those who smelt iron might have led a settled life and perhaps planted some millet, which in addition to other grains, could be the only possible plant that thrived in the open grassland. The iron tools could have been used in farm work, hunting and perhaps in war. We have no idea of any inter-tribal or any sort of war at all fought by the NOK people unless they were manufacturing the implements for neighbours and other communities around them who were engaged in long drawn battles and conflicts. It is likely that such implements constituted a big danger to continued peaceful existence of neighbouring communities. There is no trace of neighbours who lived close to the NOK people.

Smelting of iron was definitely done with fire. The technology that was applied in the process could be so local that people did not know about it. If NOK culture existed between 500 BC and 200BC as archaeologists and geologists have conservatively tried to speculate, it then means that it existed much earlier than the celebrated *Rule of Pericles* in Athens, popularly known in Ancient Greece as the *Golden Age of Doric Architecture and Beauty*. This goes to show that while the Greeks were carrying out a form of technological development that obviously improved the economy and lives of their people, a similar (but unknown to historians of the ancient times) technology and culture was growing in an obscure part of Africa- in the yet to be identified NOK Region. It is unfortunate that many people did not know about NOK culture when it actually existed during the period of Pericles in Greece. The period also fell with the epoch of Alexander the Great (332 BC – 323 BC), an age of wide conquest and expansion. By 200AD, when the NOK culture was supposed to have declined, the Emperor Constantine (306 – 337 AD) had not come to power. The Roman conquest did not extend to that part of Africa and it is hard to believe why this type of culture and civilisation remained unknown to the outside world. It is not likely to have disappeared as a result of invasions from outside Africa. If it did, it is still difficult to identify the powers that overcame it. The ancient world did not have easy communication network that could be compared with the modern world. The Ancient World was more or less concentrated in the East and Far East. It is then unlikely for historians of the period or people of the time to think of another group living in far remote areas of the West African Sub-region. The African world was a microcosm. It is no longer a surprise that no one outside the NOK region knew about them.

The earliest known *Terracotta* works of art is the only one that is of now identified with the Plateau region of that part of Northern Nigeria. Since it is peculiar to this area of Nigeria, lack of communication and contact with other parts of Africa in those days confined its influence to its local environment and consequently, other people in distant lands had no knowledge of its existence. Hence, its scope of influence and contact became limited and restricted. It is, therefore, important to note that one of the disabilities of that early skilled art and technology was the difficulty of passing knowledge to a wide range of people in distant places.

4.3   Samples from the South

The Southern Provinces of Nigeria developed a form of civilisation and culture which archaeologists have been able to unearth. Thurstan Shaw (formerly of the University of Ibadan Nigeria) and D.D. Hartle(formerly of the University of Nigeria, Nsukka) carried out a lot of valuable works independently in two different sites in Eastern Nigeria. Between 1959 and 1960, Dr Shaw did a marvellous work at Igbo-Ukwu, an apparently obscure town in Igboland. He tried to unearth a 9th Century AD Igbo civilisation. He worked with a small team of dedicated assistants who did a thorough excavation work in Igbo Ukwu. Among the objects dug out at the centre were copper and bronze equipment and tools, which depict a high level of metallurgical development. The objects from this Igbo-Ukwu site were familiar and common in this part of the world. They are like many others usually found in the Sub-Saharan Africa. The elaborate surface decorations of those ceremonial objects of copper and bronze epitomized a very high level of crafts by the artists who in their own rights could claim to be experts.

The tools were in use as commonplace domestic equipment found in royal palaces long before the people's contact with the outside world. This site is located in the hinterland of an obscure town in the Igbo heartlands.

Thurstan Shaw's excavation brought out another important ornament. There was type of pot dug out from what was supposed to be the grave of a noble king or an important wealthy chieftain. The excavated sites also represented a shrine and a storeroom, which served as a depository of the paraphernalia for some ceremonial or ritual purposes. The *Roped Pot* was cast in several pieces. It is an amazing example of an existing indigenous casting of very high quality which people had been using long before their contact with traders and travellers from outside Africa. The body of the vessel and its top as well as its bottom, the rim, etc., were part of several pieces that were cast. The knotted rope excluding the part below the last row of the knot was cast separately and then bent to fit the pot. The whole pot depicts an ornament used by dignified royal personage, an evidence of an established wealthy monarch that ruled and exercised big influence and authority over and extensive area. Such artistically cast and beautifully decorated objects could not have appeared without a strongly developed mind and fortified environment. Judging by the standard of the period, it was a magnificent technology.

Other similar ornaments found at the gravesite included large bronze bowls, snail-shell, elephant head pendant, pastoral plates, swords, and spiral snake phenomena, ram-headed pendant, leopard head pendant and other ceremonial jewellery and stools of immense values in the traditional society. Some recent anthropological studies in the area have shown that some of the materials from Igbo-Ukwu excavations are similar to those in use in the palace of the celebrated *Eze-Nri, a priest King found in the neighbouring community of Agu-Ukwu Nri.* It has been suggested that the sites where the excavations were made, were part of the *Kingdom of the legendary Igbo Priest King.*[4] A close study of Igbo traditions and myths of creation shows that the Eze-Nri was the direct descendant and successor of the first Divine Priest King believed to have been sent down from the heavens by the Supreme Deity to organise and rule the then known world of humans.

Some other archaeologists have reconstructed the Igbo Ukwu site where Thurstan Shaw worked with a team of other archaeologists. The later team concluded that in the site was a shrine or a storeroom for ritual and royal objects and regalia or probably a royal grave. A society, where such excavated ornaments were used might have been a very rich one or a community where leaders lived in luxury. If it is true as some archaeologists claim that some quantity of copper was obtained locally and the rest came from North Africa, it could be deduced that some form of trade had been going on between West and North Africa ere the Arab traders who Islamised Western Sudan arrived. It is, therefore, probable this part of West Africa in the 9th and 10th Centuries AD was not completely isolated from the other parts of Africa as has been suggested by some early European travellers and geographers. None has been able to give a precise account of the demise of such a highly complex cultural development and civilization.

It is noteworthy to make a comparative historical analysis of this epoch. The 9th and 10th centuries AD fell within the reign of Charlemagne (708 – 816 AD) and the Crusades of 1096 –1291 AD. This means that Africa had its own form of civilisation and development that prevailed during the period. Neither the Crusades nor Charlemagne's numerous conquests affected this part of Africa directly. Yet a decline of those well-established structures and civilizations had not been fully explained. Another form of highly developed material culture in Africa especially in the West African sub-region was that of Ile-Ife, which we had mentioned already. The Ife Bronze was popular throughout the whole West African sub-region. The age of the Ife Bronze fell within the 12th and 15th Centuries AD but its discovery was within the early decades of this century. Here again, the almost portrait-like appearance of the sculpture is very different from works made of bronze and terracotta. It appears stately, royal and dignifying. It is believed that they represent *the Oni of Ife, the semi divine King of Ile-Ife, the mythical cradle of human race as conceptualised by the Yoruba of Nigeria.*[5] The Bronze heads were probably placed on complete wooden bodies that were used in second burial ceremonies of the Oni. The ceremonies undoubtedly reflected the spiritual and political importance of the city-state of Ife. In the myths of the Yoruba people, Ile-Ife was the place where life began. From there, the children of the first man spread out to found their own kingdoms.[6] That man happened to be God who came to earth in human form to become the Father of all humans on earth. Where he lived at Ile-Ife became the first part of the world to be illuminated – hence Ile-Ife became known as the *House of Light* where the first divine light on earth became manifest for the good of humans who populate the universe.

Besides the Ife Civilisation, the most popular Kingdom and civilisation in the Southern Provinces in documented history, is the Benin Kingdom, Its art and culture was widely publicised in Europe by those early explorers and Slave Traders who visited Benin several times. Other reasons may be given for the wide publicity, which the Benin Monarch, art and civilisation received in history. Art aside, there are other corroborating African oral history and European travel documents which give information about Benin Kingdom.[7]

The knowledge of what existed in Benin Kingdom dates far back to the 15th century. Until the end of the 19th century, Benin was a kingdom ruled by the *Oba, another divine King widely respected by his subjects all over his extensive domain where he was regarded not only as divine but also as God's vice-regent on earth.*[8] The Portuguese missionaries and explorers who first landed in early 15th century were surprised to see the fame and influence of the Oba of Benin. The Oba was until the end of 19th century, one of the most popular and widely respected monarchs in the West African sub-region. He employed craftsmen skilled in different aspects of art to work exclusively for him. They were people who produced the magnificent works of bronze, terracotta and ivory for him. The use of bronze was the exclusive reserve of the semi divine King. It is believed that the Benin Bronze casters were taught their art from Ile-Ife around the 14th century. The court of the Benin Monarch was so attractive that the Portuguese explorers and other travellers who arrived around 1485 compared the architectural plans of the court with what they knew in their own country and concluded that Benin was really *a developed empire.* Besides that, they compared the Oba with the Pope and found him a highly respected figure in his wide empire. In consequence, they demanded to open a friendly relationship between the Oba and the Portuguese monarch. They in no way found Benin Kingdom inferior or wanting in terms of human and technological development and progress. To the surprise of the Portuguese explorers, they found out that the Oba received more respect from his subjects through out his vast empire than the Pope received in Catholic Europe.

4.4   North African Examples

It is important now that we add some models from other historic centres in Africa. Some examples from the North Africa can add credence to the claims made by a number of nationalists that Africa was culturally rich and developed long before her contact with external agents of change. Each zone had its own form of material culture, which flourished at different periods in history.

Whenever the history of the Seven Wonders of the World is mentioned in Ancient History, the Pyramid of Egypt stood out as a towering architectural structure that symbolised an apogee in human development. The Nile Valley was a *Cradle of Civilisation* in documented history. The Pyramids of Egypt can be compared with the modern sky scrappers towering into the sky in many cities of the industrialised world. The Nile Valley was a fertile region where one of the world's earliest civilizations began. A form of writing was developed in this region. It was the *Hieroglyphics*.

The papyrus reed that grew around the Nile Basin produced the parchment scrolls, which were used for writing in those days. The pyramids contained the highly sophisticated domes where the bodies of the kings and noble citizens were embalmed.

Egypt and the Nile Basin developed some flourishing centres of learning, trade and technology in the ancient world. Ptolemy and many educated mariners and geographers grew up and lived in this region. Alexandria, Cyrene, both in the Nile Basin, was among the most popular centres of Early Christianity. The Latin Bible was written in the place known today as Tunisia, a place where Christianity flourished for sometime before it was swept away by militant Islam in the 6th century AD. Many early Church Fathers were Africans or have African descent and lived within this Nile region. The School of Alexandria was a popular centre for Philosophy popularised by Philo, one of the early thinkers of the Ancient World. Men like Minucius, Felix, Tertulian, Cyprian, Arnobius, Lactantius and Augustine, among others were known to be Africans or grew up and lived in the Northern fringe of Africa, in the Mediterranean region.[9] Africa, therefore, according to many nationalists and culture historians, had played prominent roles in the formation and preservation of the Christian Church, which contributed much to the progress, *and development* of the modern world.

The glories of the Pharaohs of Egypt in the Ancient World were so obvious that one does not need to reproduce them here. It is unfortunate that some of the dynasties of the Pharaohs were of foreign pedigree and indirectly introduced many policies that did not favour the indigenous population. However, the determination of the local and indigenous people to regain ascendancy to the throne was part of the historical background to the Biblical events recorded in Exodus of the Hebrews from Egypt when a *Pharaoh who did not know Joseph came to power* The Exodus made a long-term spiritual and political impact on the life of the Hebrews. It was the Arab and the Turkish feudalism that brought the glories of Ancient Egypt to its knees.

Ethiopia, Nubia and the areas known as Kush or Meroel (location still difficult to identify) were among the famous centres of early civilization and learning in Africa. The Nubian States were believed to have achieved much from the 9th century to the 11th century AD in spite of the great devastation wrought by militant Islamic invasion, which shook the Christian Church to its roots. Kush was one of the areas that was dominated by Nubian culture and it continued to flourish even after the ascendancy of Christianity. Probably, it borrowed the growing light of Christianity and shone like a star till its light was put out by the militant Islamic attack. From Kush, it was believed that many positive cultural elements diffused to the rest of Africa. Brass work similar to the type found in West Africa was well established. It has been suggested that it was from Kush that the Brass industry in West Africa took its origin. Above all, Kush was one of the earliest and most vibrant centres of iron mining and smelting in Africa and it was certainly one of the sources from which this crucial aspect of technology passed to the rest of the continent.[10] It might be growing at the same time with the NOK culture which was known for iron-smelting as well.

The African societies so far discussed developed some form of viable commercial ventures and handicraft industries that effectively supplied them with their basic needs. We still remember the Empire of Ancient Ghana, Mali, and Songhai in the Western Sudan, now part of the West African sub-region. Ghana Empire, which began in about 5th century AD was at its peak between the 9th and 11th centuries AD. Mali was at the apogee of her own glory in the 13th and 14th centuries AD while Songhai rose to its prominence in the two subsequent centuries. They were not only noted for their commercial activities but also for rich agricultural and industrial enterprises. The gold of the Ancient Ghana was an important ornament that fetched her a lot of wealth. The gold mines found around the Upper Senegal and its tributary and the Fantene region were sources of wealth that attracted many foreigners. All these gave rise to the thriving industries that manufactured iron and brass implements for agriculture as well as for war. Works of art in wood, iron, stone, clay and bronze developed in many places too. It is really difficult to place the *Dark Ages of Africa* in its proper historical time scale if she was flouring in the distant past in many areas of life. At what point in time did Africa's local industrial establishments disappear? Many important centres grew up also in the East and Southern sub-zones of Africa. In the regions known as Zimbabwe, craftsmen who worked gold into ornaments of different sizes and shapes brought in a lot of wealth from their trade. Still, creativity and artistry were noted in the construction of the walls that were built long before European explorers like Cecil Rhodes and missionaries like David Livingston visited the region.

Conclusion

This historical analysis of the previous centres of well-developed culture in Africa has come up as a way to validate the claims that some outstanding areas of achievement did exist in some parts of the continent, ere her contact with outside visitors and explorers. This graphic representation of the features that prevailed in some of the regions points to the forms of civilisation that existed in their own forms long before any form of outside contacts were made. It has shown that although African societies were (and still) basically ethnic, many sizeable empires and kingdoms had existed and collapsed. Some African communities put up very powerful resistance against European invasion of their culture and territory. The Benin and Ashanti Kingdoms were among the early communities that built up empires of outstanding size and influence. Many other *non-monarchical and stateless societies* developed viable local industries, which manufactured war and agricultural implements that they needed. Those stateless societies existed side by side with the monarchical groups without necessarily imitating them or lacking the organisational ability and strength, which were important for peace, stability and growth. Each system developed along its own line. In spite of these recorded achievements, it is still doubtful why the glories of such immense magnitude disappeared. The next section might try to proffer some reasons.

NOTES

1. D.L. Johnson   *The Sociology of Change and Reaction in Latin America.* New York, 1976, p. 6

2. E.B. Idowu   *Olodumare: God in Yoruba Belief.* London, Longmans, 1962, pp. 20ff

3. National Museum, Lagos   *Treasures from Ancient Nigeria.* (flyers for the Exhibition). Lagos, Federal Ministry of Information, 1982

4. Thurstan Shaw   *Unearthing Igbo-Ukwu.* Ibadan Nigeria. Oxford University Press, 1977, p. 77. *An Account of Archaeological discoveries in Eastern Nigeria.* Vol. 1, London, Faber and Faber, 1970, p 267

   M.D. Jeffreys   The Umundri Tradition of Origin. *African Notes* Sept, 15th, 1956, pp. 119 – 131-61-

   M.A. Onwuejeogwu   *An Igbo Civilization: Nri Kingdom* and Hegemony. London, Ethnographica, 1980

5. E.B. Idowu   ibid, passim

   J.O. Awolalu   *Yoruba Religion and Sacrificial Rites.* London: Longmans, 1979, p. 10 – 20, 90ff.

6. J. O. Awolalu   ibid. cf. Ulli Beir, *Yoruba Myths.* London. Heinemann, 1979, p. 10 ff

7. A.F.C. Ryder   Materials for the study of African History in Portuguese Archives. London, Univ. of London Press, 1965, pp 1 – 3

8. U.R. Onunwa   The Study of African Traditional Religion in Time Perspective. Unpub PhD Thesis. Univ of Nigeria, 1984, p. 46

9. J. Ferguson   Christian Byways. Ibadan Nigeria, Day Star Press, 1967, p. 7

10. Walter Rodney   How Europe underdeveloped Africa. London 1972, p. 62

Map of Africa showing areas with strong presence of
African Traditional Religion

SECTION TWO

CHAPTER FIVE
Effects of Traditional Beliefs on Life and Development

Introduction

In the preceding chapter, we analysed a few concrete examples of material and cultural features of developments in the ancient African societies ere their contacts with external agents of change. The various forms of artefacts, which depict highly sophisticated level of cultural growth and development flourished for long time in many regions before decadence and total disappearance set in. The indigenous cultures were part of the religious systems that prevailed in those communities. It is still difficult to account for the collapse of the indigenous cultures that produced such highly developed artefacts. It is doubtful if some of them had started to deteriorate or decline before they met powerful external agent of change that finally did a dangerous blow to them. Or it was the contact with such powerful agents of change that attacked the roots of the development that could not resist the change.

We shall in this section try to adduce some reasons that might have contributed to the disappearance or collapse of such highly developed cultures and left them in ruins. The cause of the decay and eventual collapse might be many and no one single factor can explain it away. It is therefore a futile exercise to isolate one factor as the chief or only cause of the damage. Although one factor may play a prominent role in a short term or at a particular episode, a number of other factors might have contributed their roles in the long term. For instance, internal disorganisation and strife could have weakened a system before military attack by foreign invading troops routed the already weakened system.

One single factor that cannot be taken lightly in analysing the causes of the decay is the traditional religious system in which the society grew, lived and sustained itself. It is obvious that the traditional religion and culture itself contains some elements that are inherently destructive or cannot stand the test of time. It may be possible that many of the practitioners of the traditional religion could not probably identify the subtle or hidden elements inherent in their faith that could not resist the attack of an outside influence. Coupled with the negative influences of the external forces, the destructive ingredients in the traditional local cultures did not provide conducive environment for growth and continuity. This explanation does not, however, ignore the awful and horrendous effects of the solid as well as sophisticated military weapons used by western powers. The conquest of Africa by those western powers was one of the greatest misfortunes that befell the continent.

A form of development that can stand the test of time is such that is difficult to predict A. Curle has suggested an idea of development that he thought would probably suggest that the traditional African religion has some inherent traits that would constitute hindrances to the upward growth of the society. If Curle's ideas were taken on their face value, sustainable development would mean a difficult achievement for Africans. Their traditional religion and culture according to Curle, did not have the potential to sustain the form of development that would last. A lasting development means, according to him, a

Creation of a form of society in which certain conditions
Prevail for human beings-
Safety in that society is generally non-violent and that
Individuals are protected from victimisation by the State or the police or any other person.
Satisfaction- in that their lives are generously pleasant and that sufficiency is not achieved at the cost of psychological and cultural disruptions and disturbances.
Stimulus in that people are kept award of their intellectual, emotional social and spiritual potentiality and encouraged to fulfil it.[1]

The ideas of development propounded by Curle sounds too idealistic. The four conditions that would predetermine development- **safety, sufficiency, satisfaction and stimulus** are quantifiable variables. They cannot be constant in any given society. Unfortunately, the traditional African religion cannot claim to guarantee these four conditions. In many societies where Christianity has transformed the legal and ethical systems, there are built-in checks and balances that control societal norms For instance, in many traditional African societies, people carried out some religious rituals and acts of worship in good faith and as genuine and open manifestation of loyalty to the deities. For instance, human sacrifice was seen as a high and devoted service to the gods. Yet those rituals did not promote the welfare of an individual or in the long run that of the society in general. In an age of enlightenment and awareness of human rights, improvement of social values, one can look back at some of those traditional rituals and practices with nostalgia and anger.

We shall now go ahead and explore how some of the elements of the rituals in Traditional Religion, which probably did not occur to the practitioners that they were evil in themselves, blocked the chances of establishment of lasting development projects in the communities.

5.1   African Cosmology and Concept of Time

The first among the numerous features of African traditional religion and culture, which we would discuss, is the cosmology- the way Africans perceive their world. This is very important because it is a mental perception that underpins every thought and action. In other words, it is the African world-view.

Africa is vast is size and had numerous ethnic groups, each with its own tales and myths of origin and creation. The ecological differences, varieties of myths of origin and history of migration make it possible for different African peoples to perceive their world differently. Nonetheless, a synthesis of the various strands of the tales can be made, all pointing to a uniform structure and mode of thought, which characterise *small-scale primary societies.*

It is important to state that world-views are the intellectual and rational or philosophical way of explaining the order and systems, which affect or control human lives and environment in the universe. In non-classical societies, we can study people's world-views through their myths, taboos, proverbs, customs and stories that they tell. When Marcel Griaule with his team visited the Dogon of Mali, a relatively simple people in the West African sub-region, they engaged a veritable old priest, Ogotmmeli, in thirty-three days of continuous conversation. He discovered for himself what might be described Dogon world-view or perception of the world. Through the conversation, Griaule observed the underlying principles of life, which determine beliefs and practices or actions of Africans who live in Dogon community. He used that model as a paradigm for other African communities.[2] His background from the *French School* made him begin from *a philosophical theory to action* instead of starting from *functions to theory*, of the **British School** model. He later concluded that African traditional religion and culture is not merely a reflection of the socio-economic system but an autonomous way of thought and action. From this inference, one can state that a world-view is a unified picture of the cosmos explained by systems of concepts, which order natural and social rhythms and the place of individuals and communities in them.[3]

A cosmology is and intellectual and rational construct that is based on two most important experiences of *time* and *space*. The structure of the African world can be perceived from the various *beings* that occupy the *Three-Decker compartment* of the universe that the people project. There is an implication of pointing to the sky above as the abode of the Supreme Being and some other major divinities, which we discussed in Chapter Three. The earth is inhabited by the Earth-goddess and other nature divinities; patron deities of human activities and ecology. Here is the visible world in which human beings, animals and plants created by God live. The third segment is *the Invisible World* (the Other World) – often described as the *World Beneath*. This is believed to be the abode of the departed human spirits, the ancestors and other dismembered sprits. Humans live in the middle compartment hanging between the upper and lower compartments. Human world literally *hangs in balance*. It hangs between the world above and that beneath. Both are invisible. This makes the human world a *precarious universe*. One must be careful and cautious in order to live happily and safely in it. It is a universe full of difficulties, hardships and dangers. Without caution, life on earth is dangerous. Humans can exercise this caution by living pure, clean and righteous life, respecting the deities and obeying their laws, respecting the elders and offering necessary rituals and sacrifices when due. In spite of the dangers that one encounters in the universe, life on earth is still worth the risk. There is a regular *rhythm* and *order*. The universe moves in an *ordered cycle*. If this order is disrupted through bad living or misbehaviour, the system would collapse and humans who live in it would suffer.

In a cyclical universe, the day follows the night, life comes after death, and rainy season follows the dry one in an ordered sequence. A notion of *inseparable duality* pervades the thought-pattern of humans, thus making good and evil, man and woman, white and black, tall and short, night and day, light and darkness, young and old, etc., form complementary pattern of existence. This gives a rhythm of life, a *sequence* of one event after the other, symbolising harmony, consistency and dynamism. A disruption of this order and harmony would bring disaster to humans who live in the *precarious universe*. There is, therefore, an ethical implication in maintaining this harmony and avoiding the attendant dangers that follow misconduct. An offending traditional priest could be struck by an inexplicable thunder. A falling tree or a wild animal while walking on the road could kill him. The precarious nature of the universe brings religion to the core of the world-view. Humans living on earth use the religion do three basic things- **explanation,** of how, when and why things happen; **prediction** of what would follow an action, and **control** of events in the universe to suit human needs and convenience.

E.E. Evans-Pritchard had discovered among the Nuer people of Sudan, that seasons and monthly changes repeat themselves year after year in *a cyclical order*. The moon becomes instrumental in calculating changes in seasons.[4] This is the system in many African societies. On the other hand, Mircea Eliade saw the continuity and cyclical repetition of events and seasons in nature among preliterate and simple societies as the *Myth of Eternal Return*.[5] In those societies, one event repeats itself in a cyclical and continuous order and returns after a set period of time.

Taking this cyclical view of the universe a little further, John Mbiti discusses the traditional concept of time in a very strikingly controversial manner. African peoples calculate events within a perceptible universe in relation to two principal factors of time and space. He raised the issue of the absence of a distant future in African method of time reckoning. He discovered a two-tier time dimension- the *present and the past* and virtually an absence of a *distant future*. Apart from nationalism, Mbiti used traditional events, profession, language and other ethnographic data to explain how Africans calculate time. He did not deserve the adverse criticisms he received because he was both objective and analytical in his presentation. He is the first indigenous African scholar to look at time from a continental perspective and should be commended for his pioneering work. According to him:

> *Time as a separate reality, does not move; only events come and go, often in a rhythmic succession. It is therefore, what has taken place shortly that matters much more than what is yet to be...Time as a succession or simultaneity of events moves not forward but backwards. People look more to the past for the*

orientation of their being than to anything that might yet to come into human history.[6]

Although Mbiti did not discuss *space* in his analysis of *time* (both are inseparable phenomenon), he was not properly understood by many of those who criticised his views. In a sense, if he was properly understood, or had expressed his ideas more clearly, what he was struggling to say was that it is not time that *moves* into the past but *events* do. For instance, in most African societies, those who criticised Mbiti, know very well that time does not exist apart from human activities. It is man's activities that *create time*. Since time is created by human activity, the distant future contains no events to be spoken of. An indefinite distant future is thus *atrophied*, not because the people cannot calculate it or reckon it as useless, but primarily because they do not have any event to place within its spectrum. It is not because the means of reckoning it is not there, but because the *distant future is unreal and unrealised as it contains no events*. Consequently, it has not been brought into the realm of human activity. *It has not yet been humanized.*

We ought to place the discussion of time reckoning in Africa within its historical and contextual position. The Greek term- *chronos*- meaning lineal time is used in many industrialized Western societies. We hear of such terms like *chronology, chronometer*, which are related to straight-line method of time reckoning. This system does not apply to non-industrialised simple societies. The appropriate Greek term for primary and agrarian non-industrialised societies is *Kairos*, which means *seasons*. Events in the natural world move in cyclical order and repeat themselves. We must understand this before we embark on any meaningful discussion on African methods of time reckoning.

African date events or incidents in relation to other spectacular ones that took place before of after them. They do not talk *of time in abstract mathematical* figures. Mbiti tried to explain this and obviously emphasized the fact when he stated that *there is no strong projection of a distant future in African method of time reckoning*. E. E. Evans-Pritchard noted the same thing among the Nuer of Sudan when he stated that people refer to outstanding events or activities in interpreting others.[8] If an African is asked his age or his date of birth, he does not state a particular mathematical day of the month and year. The best he could do is to tell the important events or incidents that took place in his community or neighbouring community or the country during the period. He is not precise but gives the events that took place within the period. Africans have good memories and as such can remember the details of the events. Consequently, it is difficult for an African to tell his age with a mathematical precision and accuracy because his people do not calculate time in that way. People born within a period of time, often between a gap of three to five years, are usually lumped together into one *Age Group* though every woman knows whose baby arrived first and tells her child so. One is, therefore, never ignorant of one's older or younger colleague in the community when peers meet.

People use natural phenomena and events in community to calculate the traditional calendar. The seasons of the year feature prominently in the calculation of the days, month (phases of the moon) and the year. The appearance of the moon, stars, etc., depicts the regularity of the seasons. The year is divided into two equal parts, - the Dry Season (depicting death and harvest) and the Rainy Season (depicting Life and Resurrection). Thus a cyclical order of the universe is maintained and events take place at their appropriate seasons- planting and harvesting, sleeping and waking, living and dying, etc.

Meetings are usually fixed or scheduled before or after a particular human activity, which is often determined by the movement of natural phenomenon. For instance, the day is calculated by the rising and setting of the sun and the month is calculated by the phases of the moon in the sky. At every stage of the sun's movement, one human activity or the other is taking place. The time to go to the farm, to fish, to tap the wine in the morning, afternoon, night, is determined by the location of the sun on its movement in the sky. The time to milk the cow and the time to come back from the market, etc, will be clear to all who live in a community that uses the sun to calculate time. The sun casts human shadow, which either lengthens or shortens according to the position of the sun. Time is Africa, therefore, is *humanized and relational* – (i.e. related to human activity). It is *humanised in* the sense that no one speaks of abstract time unless it is in relation to such *human activities* like farm work, fishing, tapping of wine, wrestling, festivals, etc. Africans therefore, do not conceptualise time in the same way the West do. To those in the West, time moves in *a continuum or lineal order*, from past to present, then slips into the future in a straight line. To the Africans, the seasons of the year repeat in an eternal cycle. It is in this order that events come and go. It is the fact, which makes the perception of a distant future- beyond six months – a little problematic for one who is used to the

Western notion of time. For instance, since the next season is envisaged soonest within six months, it is not seen as something far away because it will soon succeed the present one. It can then be thought of and calculated. Larger period of time is often calculated by some people in terms of successive age sets that were born within specific given period of time of about three to five years. Short future periods are easily calculated especially when one goes to borrow money or materials from a neighbour but ordinarily, an indefinite projection of a distant future of about ten years is atrophied. This is exactly what Mbiti was struggling to express and which is obvious to any one who has come close to the elders and custodians of the traditional society. Mbiti's work was the first comprehensive effort by an indigenous African scholar to look at the religion at a continental level and should be commended.

From experience gained through personal contacts in the field with many living votaries of the traditional religion, the present writer has come to understand that they have the tendency to account backwards when some great events take place. Often they continue to refer to great events that took place in the life of the community in the past. For instance, the death of a king, the coronation of a new king, inter or intra village war, etc. continue to be a reference term in African time calculation. This obviously assimilated the future into the past. For instance, many elders continuously refer to the old good days, implying the period when things were in order, the age of innocence. The elders continue to refer to the past when humans were at peace with divine. The diviner peers into the rich and glorious past to seek explanations for the misfortunes of the present and what to do to avoid it in the future that contains no event. It is the past that is full of events. Obviously, the orientation of a typical African is towards the past which eventually reappears through the process of the cyclical concept of the universe into what is called *the future*. The past points to the ancestors who had lived and on whose legacies their successors depend. It is on the ancestors that their children cling for support in a precarious universe. No doubt scientists have wondered whether the materialistic conception of time prevalent in Africa hinders *development theory and innovation in the physical sciences.*[9]

In chapter three, we discussed the various beings that occupy the African pantheon. That of space complements the concept of time. Within the tree compartments of the universe, are Spiritual Beings, which are either friendly or hostile to human existence and progress here on earth. God is not primarily at the centre of man's worship. All the good habits and actions which humans enjoin are primarily aimed at making the visible world liveable and comfortable for them and their fellows and not necessarily to glorify God. Human orientation is towards life on earth and hence African world-view is *life- affirming*, and *world affirming* not *life renouncing* and *world-renouncing*. Human efforts are geared towards maintaining a clean and stable society where people could enjoy life in abundance and return to, after death, through the *process of reincarnation* and continue another series of sojourn. The notion of the present world of human life or human world ending one day is completely strange to the Africans. There is no concept of it in any of the African myths, which the present writer has been able to analyse. This is one of the consequences of a mental frame of thought that is *cyclical* which does not show an end to the cycle. The world continues to go round and round in a cycle. The idea of *eschatology* is conspicuously lacking in African cyclical way of thinking. The African conceives of the idea of Reincarnation in which life flows in a cycle of births and rebirths and therefore death is not seen as a terminus but as a portal to another life in the spirit world which opens again into the human world for another cycle of sojourn. It is note worthy that the concept of reincarnation is not peculiar to Africa but is also found among many other non-classical and simple societies. The operational system of the idea of reincarnation may however differ from one community to the other but it is a reflection of a cyclical concept of the universe.

In African ideas of reincarnation, the personality soul continues to live in the Spirit World until it reincarnates into the human world in the form of a little baby. The spirit world is a mirror of the human world with the same topography and social organization. Thus, the ancestors are often referred to as the *living dead who though dead in this world, are alive in the Spirit World.*[10]

It is believed that a wealthy man on earth would retain his exalted social status in the spirit world while a poor man retains his humble position too. This explains certain bizarre funeral rites that people carry out in some communities. For instance, a local chieftain may be buried with a large retinue including slaves, one of his beautiful wives, who would serve him in the spirit world. It may surprise one to learn that some members of a late man's family may struggle to be chosen among those to be buried with him. For the African traditional religious votaries, there were none of the egalitarian hopes of resurrection, which Christianity offers all believers and sojourners on earth.[11]

The belief in reincarnation can be taken a little further as a symbolic demonstration of the belief in life after death. It is one of the cardinal African doctrines revitalizing the notion that the end is not sealed at death. It is important to note that the concept is a philosophical explanation for lineage identity and continuity as well as an effort to defeat death. Humans regard death as an intruder and a dangerous enemy, which tries to disrupt the highest value in the world- life.

Through the process of reincarnation, the respected ancestors seek re-entry from the spirit world back into the human world of time and space in the children that are born into the families. The number of children born into the lineage in a particular year determines the number of ancestors who would return to their kiths and kin through reincarnation. The responsibility of creating the viable conditions for the return of the ancestors lies in the hands of their progeny. Such conditions include befitting burial and funeral rites, viable descent group, etc. We have already discussed part of the conditions for canonisation of an ancestor in Chapter Three.

The desire for children in Africa has a far more important religious significance than the sociological and demographic implications. It is one of reasons for polygamy practised in many communities in Africa. African ideas of marriage and procreation automatically condemn celibacy and childless marriage. A childless marriage is not consummated and could be terminated as useless and valueless because it has in no way enhanced the chances of the ancestors to come back to life through the babies that would have been born into the families. Celibacy, on the other hand, is seen as a contradiction of the ideal state of life, rank foolishness and a calculated effort to close down the lineage by blocking the chances of the ancestors to reincarnate into the families. Single persons are treated with contempt and spite, and their refusal or failure to marry is regarded as an incredible upsetting of the social and religious order. Through the children who are born into the family or lineage, the society faces the challenge of death and preserves its fading image. The continuous supply of children reassures the African that his lineage will not close down.

It is on this basis that many Africans still find it difficult to appreciate the western view of family planning. It is seen as a wilful and selfish attempt to enjoy life, avoid responsibility and block the chances of many ancestors from returning to enjoy life in this visible world of *time and space*. This had led to the refusal of many Africans to reduce the number of children they can have in spite of harsh economic conditions. Over production of children or the desire to have many wives should be understood in its proper context. It is not because of the people's inability to live sexually disciplined lives or to practise the virtue of chastity and continence. It is rather a high sense of responsibility and obligation to God, community and the ancestors. This is one of the reasons for the GDP of many African countries ranking lowest in the world. The increase in population is not matched with increase in food production, adequate housing and job creation. In *un- dislocated* African societies, food, housing and jobs were never in short supply. People had enough of all that they needed until money economy introduced by the West ripped them off of their sources of wealth. The pathetic sight of hungry-looking, naked, sick women and children lying on the street corners begging food in many African cities and villages have become constant images for Charities and other Aid Organisations in the West for fund raising. This is a typical picture of under-*development* in contemporary period.

The *Upper Segment* of the universe is believed to be the abode of the Supreme Being and some other divinities like the moon, sun, the god of Thunder as we have already stated in chapter three. Man does not expect himself to go up and dwell there with them. The heavenly beings that dwell there often come down to the human world to commune with humans and at times harass them. Ritual sacrifices are offered to placate the angry gods as well as to seek the favour of the friendly ones. In African world-view, human beings (humanity) are at the centre of the universe. They see themselves as the focal point of all creation. This creates a notion of self-importance in man (anthropos) in such a way that in Africa, human beings invite God and the divinities to come down to him to bless him on earth. He does not plead with God to take him up to the Sky or Heaven where the Supreme God dwells. This traditional theological concept has to be properly understood, as it is a strong determinant of human behaviour on earth. Man makes his home on earth, plants his food there, and at death is buried in the soil, only to return through the process of reincarnation to begin a new sojourn and adventure. He inevitably becomes a *persistent and stubborn earth-dweller*. The visible earth surface becomes the big arena of human activity where he lives out his life. This does not mean that he does not believe in the existence of the spirit world.

Although other created beings dwell in the universe, humans think that those other beings live to serve them. Any situation, which does not favour humanity, becomes *inhuman* and is usually condemned in strong terms. Humans assess the validity and value of any phenomenon, policy or transaction by its level of utility to human convenience and comfort. Although humans pray to God and other deities, they tend to use *those beings* as means to create a suitable earthly environment for human existence. The African world, from all indications, can be described as *anthropocentric* and not *theocentric It is a world which humans are at the centre of the universe.* This does not make man manipulative of the deities but African religious worldview can be said to be teleological and in some ways utilitarian.

5.2   Implications of the world-view for development

African concept of time is quite different from Western ideas based on lineal and abstract mathematical calculation. The use of the sun or moon for calculating time does not in any way give the sense of precision in time reckoning. One is at the mercy of the natural phenomena to know when to embark on a project. On a rainy day, for instance, the sun may not be out to give an accurate idea of when to begin or when to stop a job. No matter how the users adjust to be productive, in comparative terms, it will be difficult for the output to match those of a scientific process. One of the weaknesses of African (and in fact every primary society) civilization is its inability to pay special attention to *chronometric system* of time reckoning. There is a very serious defect in the way time is calculated in Africa, which people humorously describe as *African Time*, which is a euphemistic way of describing a very serious weakness in a productive economy if time is to be a strong determinant in wealth creation. Starting a meeting one-hour late means working with *African time.* Any society which does not understand the long term effect of the loss of one minute by fifty people in an industry will find it difficult to survive or establish a lasting industrial and economic business. The inability to check misuse of many productive hours has led to huge financial losses in many modern African enterprises.

Many young people wasted their prime in the village loitering till they embarked upon viable economic venture late in life. This is because many Africans do not count their ages with mathematical figures. Often, an African cannot easily count numerals in his local language beyond a few hundreds. A large crowd of about five hundred people is often described as *uncountable*. One who is not precise in calculation of figures can hardly project any large sized business enterprise. Time and specific calculation of figures are factors *of economic development and growth*. Yet, these two factors do not mean much to an African in his village planning how to get along with his work in the year. The non-projection of an indefinite future in Africa has in a subtle way, affected even some educated Africans in positions of leadership in their various countries. Those of them who should plan ahead for the development of their countries do not apply the principles of precise statistical figures in their planning. Consequently, many have not been able to plan for and establish major economic projects that will be of benefit to the country in the next hundred years or so. They are handicapped by the thought-pattern that shaped *the traditional microcosmic world-view*.

It is sad to observe that many people in leadership positions lack the ability to project ahead for a solid future. Some critics have explained the failure of many African leaders to build up their countries in terms of corruption that is endemic in their political systems. That may not be the whole truth. Yes, there is corruption everywhere. But one must not lose sight of the traditional religious world view which formed the people's thought pattern and still affect and determine their trends of thought in a very subtle way. There are many well and honest leaders in Africa who are not corrupt per se but lack the foresight *to project a macro-world and indefinite future*. Some distressing examples can be cited from the on-going projects in some countries of Africa. For instance, some of the new roads under construction are so narrow that one doubts if the leaders understand the rate of growth of population and the volume of traffic in the next five years in some of the urban centres. So it is with some classroom blocks, hospitals, markets, stadiums, theatres, and other public utilities being built in different countries with high rate of population growth estimated at about 1.6% per year.

The problem in many African countries today is not necessarily lack of money or corruption, as some people seem to emphasise. Lack of money coupled with corruption cannot, however, be ignored. Yet lack of ability to plan for the effective use and distribution of available resources had led to the current decay and underdevelopment. The inability is traceable to the absence of ways to project a distant future in the traditional culture inherited by the people including those in leadership positions. Some of the technical hitches people experience at the airports, railway stations, telephone stations, hotels, banks, post offices, hospital theatres, etc, are inherited from a traditional way of thinking and planning that does not project and indefinite future. Many African economic planners do not even think of the state of the economy by the year 2050! It sounds like a fable to them.

Many good roads do not last up to five years before they begin to crumble. If repairs, replacements of broken-down slabs and gutters are projected and provisions for them effectively supplied, no one would run into the type of problems that African countries go through. One thing is to erect a good building and the other is to plan for its long-term maintenance and upkeep. Many Africans may not accept this explanation. We shall, however, come back to it when we discuss the effects *of microcosmic* nature of the African world. Constant power cuts in many cities in Africa can be remedied if contingent funds are set aside to buy spare parts to repair broken down and unserviceable machines. Unfortunately, some but many planners do not project into the distant and indefinite future to anticipate that such machines would one day break down due to age, over use and other unexpected breakdowns.

The microcosmic worldview, which prevails in Africa, is too narrow to project far into the future. It is this microcosmic worldview that has made some African scholars doubt the ability of the Africans to conceptualise a Supreme Being. Besides, it is becoming increasingly difficult for many African leaders to manage the size of the population in their countries. The population and size of some countries are becoming too vast and large, too multi-cultural, and too complex for a man whose worldview is confined to his ethnic boundaries to lead. Many federal governments are becoming too complex for effective management. Many tribal leaders were transformed into multi-ethnic and national leaders overnight. This was a task many of them had not been spiritually and emotionally prepared to handle.

Besides the problem of time, a society where all misfortunes, including natural and ecological disasters are explained by the agency of the *ubiquitous evil spirit- the devil* may end up living helplessly at the mercy and fear of *non-existent beings*. Any group of people, whose philosophy of life is shaped in that way, may lack the enquiring and adventurous minds to probe and explore the unknown universe. No one in such societies would like to take risks. Consequently, they may not be able to develop to the full, all human potentials within them and obviously could not attempt to explore the natural resources within their environments. Humans living in such societies would continue to tug at the apron string of the *benevolent nature*. Superstition can becloud any one's mind and hinder exploration into the unknown.

Furthermore, a society with a world-view in which bizarre funeral rites are performed to placate angry gods and ancestors or to enhance a dead man's status in the Spirit World could face a lot of problems *of development of individual talents and potentials*. Any young person can be used for some sordid ritual sacrifices if captured at night by a gang of ritual experts or by their tugs that go about hunting for human heads that would be used for sacrifices. Such traditions and practices could place every one in a psychological state of uncertainty and fear, especially when a local chieftain dies and the funeral obsequies are to be performed.

5.3   Peculiarities of Traditional Religion and Culture (Their Implications for Development)

The African world is a microcosm. That implies that a person's whole life perception is conceptualised and concentrated on the enclave in which he lives and will spend all his life. Both time and space for a person born within microcosmic environs are too narrow and small for any meaningful projection of his work to benefit a wider society. Surprisingly, when a person is told of another group of people or race living in the world, it does not bother him to go and explore who they are and how they look like or what they do. Because the African world is a microcosm, the religion and culture become too localised and ethnic. The gods become local heroes, heroines, patrons and champions of the people's course. The welfare of every compartment of life within the community becomes the preoccupation of the local deities. The gods of the other communities are there for them too. There was no documented or literary tradition to project or defend the identity and integrity of the religious culture that shaped African cosmology. The religion was therefore ethnic and folk in nature. This utter lack of sense of literary and durable classical documentary records hindered development, projection and preservation of technological inventions whenever any was made. Any incursion from outside could sweep off some salient aspects of a folk religion and tradition.

There is no reference written source. African religion and culture, therefore, operated within very restricted horizon and only met effectively the needs of the face to face rural communities of pre-colonial Africa.[12] Robin Horton has elsewhere, described the pre-colonial African life as a way of life…dominated by subsistence farming in which social relations are likely circumscribed by the boundaries of the local microcosm and which produces a religious life in which a great deal of attention is paid to the lesser spirits, underpinners of the microcosm.[13]

The microcosmic frame of thought prevalent in the traditional African society invariably influenced people's action and restricted their movement and projection of long-term programmes. Such microcosmic environment that shaped and nurtured the traditional religion and culture restricted people's scope in life's adventure and attainment. It could not enhance growth of interaction with people from other ethnic groups, races and countries. It could not encourage growth of self-awareness up to a certain limit. There is a growth of self-awareness when men and women move from isolated preliterate communities and the most important factor in this growth is the ability to communicate.[14]

In small and microcosmic societies, members have great difficulties in conceptualising the group and analysing relationships in them. Men in very isolated society scarcely reflect on their institutions. But the study of society is a condition of existence for modern *and macrocosmic society* and a necessity for intervention and expansion. The growth of knowledge and skill is the mark of a large society. The traditional African society, therefore, lacked the inherent qualities and propensities for growth in knowledge and skill, hence the *underdevelopment* that set in after a short time of apparent success and growth that could not last for a long time. Even the Benin and Ashanti Kingdoms, which we discussed in Chapter three, among other African Kingdoms that flourished in pre-colonial Africa and enlarged their territories by conquest, could not go far enough. They later began to decline probably because of their traditional perception of the world and inability to cope with vast and expansive pressure of work and management that come from multi-ethnic and multi-cultural encounters. The problem created by non-projection of a distant future and the prevalence of microcosmic world-view is not starting a project but continuing and sustaining it for a long time when it begins to expand. Many African countries started laudable projects like running commercial airlines, free medical and educational programmes, welfare scheme, etc which took off beautifully but collapsed after a few years.

Monica Wilson, an outstanding anthropologist has aptly summarised the problem of small-scale societies, which were modelled on the perception of the traditional religion and culture. It is noted from her observations that:

> within the last two hundred years men have looked back nostalgically to small-scale societies. Rousseau wrote of the noble savage. Some today seem to seek an anarchy- an absence of organization which would take us back to a small-scale existence. Those who praise the small-scale societies have rarely lived in them, in isolation for long... Those who hanker after primitive life have not understood the implications- a world without books, a world in much sickness without effective medicine; a world without transport in which famine threatens, for where there is isolation, bad weather spells starvation; a world of sameness since hunter or cultivator enclosed in his own tiny community does not savour that variety which entrances the outsider visiting one isolated society and then another.[15]

It is difficult to place the above observation into its historical context. In spite of its exaggerations, it reveals partially the true situation of what life in rural communities looked like in the past. It is not true anyway to say that there was isolation in rural communities that were closely knit and people knew their neighbours and kiths and kin. Life in primary societies had its own dangers but they were not exposed to the greed and tension of modern and industrialized societies where *anomie and rugged individualism* have brought human life under serious tension. Travelling which is a part of education and enlightenment was grossly reduced in primary societies. A society in which people could not travel far and wide hindered their chances to interact with others as well as borrowing ideas from them. Most people were unfortunately confined to their local environs for life. A society in which most of the inhabitants are indigenes, born and bred within the area, could hardly provide sufficient wide-range of opportunities and challenges needed for development. No society is so self-sufficient that it does not need the contributions of people from other places to assist or contribute to its *development*. In effect, development should be seen as a collective effort of people and not an isolated lone achievement of a people or person.

5.4   Traditional Work Ethics

The range of *moral obligations* was very narrow in small-scale societies. The Christian idea of neighbourhood is both radical and inclusive. It is a radical deviation from traditional preconceived idea and experience of who a neighbour is. It is a radical interpretation and understanding of the narrow view of help in traditional and primary non-industrialised society. With enlargement of scale, African societies became radically transformed. There is visible all around us the conflict between extending interaction and the refusal to acknowledge *the other person* who is different as a neighbour. The answer given by Jesus to the question, **who is my neighbour?**-is an inclusive one, involving the Samaritan, the outsider, the outcast, the person from the other race, gender, social class, people with different ideological, political, religious and economic principles, etc (Luke 10: 25 – 42). I am a neighbour *to one who is in need, any time, any place and any how.* The fact that a Samaritan was presented to be a neighbour in a community, which though a colony of Rome, was in no way yet part of the world society, is not only challenging but also refreshing.

In Elizabethan England, many thought it right to put the interest of kinsmen before that of the State. In many African societies, it is still the norm. Along with the extension of the range of moral obligations, there is a growth of individual freedom from immediate kin and neighbours. This may, however, have some subtle negative influences if not properly addressed and directed For instance, it may lead to *rugged individualism*, (as it unfortunately has done in some places), a disregard for the needs of others or to a narrow parochialism which destroys the progress of the entire society.

Many scholars think African religion and culture lacks clear theological concept of sin. They base their argument on the fact that customs and traditions form African behaviour. Prohibitions, taboos and customs characterize the African traditional form of morality.[16] People do not base their morality on proper conviction that a particular behaviour is wrong or right but on the idea that – *it is the way we do it.* The scholars who hold this view of African morality insist that Africans do not make direct reference to God when sin is committed nor do they see it as a direct offence against God. An offence is not a disobedience to God's law but a violation of the customs of the society. It is the *society itself* that enacted the rules of conduct to hold rebellion-prone humans in check. This is the view of Emile Durkheim, who invariably tried to make *the Society,* the real god the people worship.

Some other scholars saw African culture as one that is *shame-oriented* and not *guilt-oriented.* This, in other words, means that people avoid doing evil because of the shame they suffer and not because of the guilt involved. Those who project this view believe that the *summum bonum* (the greatest good) of the Africans is the enjoyment of life and public esteem and not a quiet conscience. This goes to confirm that the greatest moral force in a *shame culture* is *respect from the public* and not the *evenness of mind* from doing right.

Some indigenous African Christian theologians like Francis Arinze, Harry Sawyer and Edmund Ilogu see African concept of sin as a violation of authority, not of the Supreme God per se but that of the spirits and ancestors.[17] This view must not be taken completely in its face value. Robin Horton had earlier stated that a great deal of attention is paid to the lesser spirits in the local microcosm. J.V. Taylor came up later to confirm that African moral concept is shame oriented and not guilt-oriented.[18] John Mbiti whom we had earlier discussed stated that African traditional religion and culture, has no clear concept of sin.[19] In all, there is some element of shame and guilt in what many Africans perceive as sin. The idea of conscience is not strange to an African and he often fears when his conscience is pricking him and he feels ashamed of meeting one hurt.

Traditional African morality can be said to be teleological in the sense that a community insists that social actions and relationships must be guided by the considerations that the moral purpose of the universe must be maintained by such actions. Thus individual good is often underplayed and neglected when an act is thought of as a threat to the security of the entire community. One's right to existence is meaningful only within the context of that of the entire community. It is against this background that many ritual killings and human sacrifice, (which we have already mentioned), rampant in traditional societies, were seen as legitimate actions by the practitioners of the traditional religion. The interest of the society was considered supreme while the freedom of the individual was only a function of it. The individual comes and goes but the community remains. So no single individual is greater than the entire community. No individual has the right to challenge the decisions of the community, however obnoxious and oppressive they might be. The rights of an individual are not emphasized if they are considered a danger to the life of the entire community. This posture was taken to the extreme and left the individual totally miserable and helpless in the hands of dictators and tyrants who destroyed their opponents in the pretext of defending the rights of the community which they represent.

Some field research workers might often hear of *the perfect moral standard that existed in traditional African societies before the advent of corrupting influences of the West.* That might be true to some extent because the *un-dislocated African societies* held some moral norms that have now been broken. For instance, people had their reasons for not committing adultery openly or secretly- either because of fear of being caught and disgraced, or fear of being struck dead by the clan deity. People who grew up with that type of moral training and orientation became afraid of doing wrong primarily to avoid the awful consequences and not because *the action was intrinsically evil.* Any smart person who knew any escape route could commit atrocities without being caught and without pricking of conscience. Most of the time, ethics *of fear* prevailed and operated in the traditional society. The slogan, *don't be found out,* became the watchword of *many smart crooks* that transgressed the rules of the society.

A society that approved or casually winked at the sin of abuse of the rights of an individual citizen could obviously not provide the basis for the development of *the individual gifts and talents* which any community would need for its holistic growth. Gross injustice was perpetrated in many ways and clever people paid highly for it because they expressed individual opinion on some matters that the community felt highly irritated. It was a matter of collective opinion whether the individual was right or not.

A subtle dysfunctional effect of this form of traditional ethics is its *indifference to the good of the* other *community.* The other community may be good neighbours but people praised their kinsmen when they stole *from the other community but* not from their own kinsmen. A community could honour such thieves for being clever and strong. There was *no moral absolute* in the ethical law of many traditional societies. The structure of the **Apodictic Laws**- thou *shall not*... or *do not*...was not totally present in many traditional societies. Some people treated certain acts as sinful or evil only when those acts were directed against them. For instance, it was evil to steal from a kinsman or kill a kinsman. If it was directed to people in another community, they could at best be treated casually or lightly condemned. We have noticed that some traditional societies followed a form of **Casuistic Proviso** in their rules of norms especially when they affect people from another community. An elder from one village confirmed this. Their ethical rules run thus:

> *Do not steal... especially from your kinsmen*
> *Do not commit adultery... especially with a kinsman's wife*
> *Do not kill... especially a relative.*

This implies that when a person kills a non-kinsman, the offence is not as heavy as when a kinsman is affected. A man who stole the foreigner's property would be applauded for being brave and courageous.

This was the background to the general attitude of many Africans toward government during the heyday of colonial administration. It is unfortunate that this was carried over into post independence era when the people themselves ran the national government. This is the background to the endemic corruption and wanton destruction of public property in many African countries. The basic corruption has increased the rate of political instability and the difficulty of building stable democracy. Civil service is still described in the local language of many African ethnic groups as White man's job- the *business enterprise belonging to the European colonisers*. Many civil servants still hold the erroneous views that they are working for foreign employers especially where the national government is insensitive to the plight of its poor workers and citizens. The colonial administration has its blame in laying such a weak foundation that passed on to the nationals at the dawn of independence. It was an awful heritage.

The prevailing double standards of morality are not helping to build a clean and vibrant society. The praise and commendation, which a man received from his kinsmen for successfully robbing a public treasury, is an indication of a type of citizenry that has not been made to understand the meaning of patriotism and nationalism. One cannot talk of patriotism in the midst of poor people who do not benefit from the government of their countries. Although elaborate enlightenment programmes on moral and ethical orientation are going on in many countries, it has been difficult to change the old system inherited from the colonial days. Since many national governments have not been able to run effective systems that can convince their citizens that the new administration is not an extension of the erstwhile colonial powers in local dresses, ordinary people will continue to see governments as properties of the enemy from which they can steal if they had the chance.

The extended-family system, which is a bye-product of small-scale society, has created an enormous problem of large-scale bribery and corruption in many African countries. It may have some useful role to play in making one look after his kinsmen, especially when one is rich and comfortable. Yet it is one of the causes of the temptation for one in public office to look for money by all means to assist a long line of poor relatives looking for support. Some jobs are offered to unqualified persons because they are related to the managers or those in top positions in the department. A lot of partiality is going on in the employment sector because the leaders want to offer the few existing jobs to their own kinsmen or people from their ethnic groups. All these are problems caused by the *microcosmic worldview of Africans.*

Many countries in Africa are the creations of the colonial powers that ruled them. People who had nothing in common and are in no way homogeneous were compelled by a foreign agent to come together for his own interest. There was no mutual agreement on terms of relationship. In many places, it was a *marriage of incompatible bedmates.* This speaks clearly for the constant inter-ethnic rivalry, wars, and political instability in many modern African countries, which were creations of the colonial administration. Instability would continue until a mutual basis for co-existence is found. We must understand the religious background to this. No one would entrust his life or destiny to a person who worships another god. Each community has its own god that looks after it. It is suicidal to pledge and entrust yourself to the protection of the god of another community by letting a man from there to act as your leader. This contradicts the religious faith of each community, which had never been enslaved or ruled by another group at all. African concept of democracy is quite different from what it is in the West. For the African, it implies religious, cultural and economic control of the people's life. Some African tribal groups see it as a new form of slavery for their people to allow a leader from another religious or ethnic group to rule them and determine their fate, control their economy, gods and future.

Nationalism or patriotism is still a vague term in many African countries. It really means love for one's kindred or at best ethnic group. This is one's largest scope of security. This is primarily based on the concept of the area of the Shades of the ancestral cult in primary society. Many people may not see it that way or pretend that it is not so but it is the basic determinant of one's notion of security and sphere of obligation. Basically, if we critically analyse the world of a typical African, whether literate or illiterate, simple of sophisticated, rural or urban, it is a microcosm – his close-knit community that is the context of his security and development. The gods of his fathers do not act beyond the confines of their limited sphere of authority. In modern time, this notion has unconsciously been transferred to the areas of politics, education, economics, marriage and every other aspects of life.

Since no society is static, African worldview must grow. If this is going to happen, the new national governments must act in such a way that every citizen would see the larger country as his own microcosm in which his security, economy, faith, ancestors, etc are secure. If he finds security in the large community, which now acts as his country, he would transfer his traditional loyalty from the microcosmic ethnic community to the national government, which gives him his new identity. This is the extension of scale and growth of the shades.

The objective analyst who sees development in terms of improvement of human and natural resources would agree that the endemic ethnic (tribal) loyalty and interest of many Africans established on their microcosmic worldview and sustained by the traditional religion is a factor of underdevelopment. If African countries can treat all their citizens in such a way that they see themselves as part of the national system, they can enlarge their microcosm to macrocosm and think globally but live locally. The development of technology and stable democracy as well as economy would then emerge as a new way of life.

In conclusion, Chinua Achebe has in a pungent analysis of the problem of Africa thrown the gauntlet to all who aspire to make the continent develop and grow. In his little but powerfully written book, which sounds *like an advocacy for social reform or a declaration of a new social order,* Achebe did as it were, an anatomy of the diseases of the Third World Nations that inherited a truncated alien legacy which cannot stand on a weak ethnic foundation.[20] When an appointment to the headship of any of the top government institutions and establishments like the universities, armed forces, banks and industries is based on a candidate's ethnic origin, one begins to doubt whether such a country would ever understand the true meaning and implications of *development*. The religious factor that has shaped the idea of the microcosm that has kept Africa down must be discarded if genuine development would be experienced in this generation. The society is growing and must overcome this bottleneck.

NOTES

1. A. Curle — *Education for Liberation. (London: Tavistock, 1973), p. 118-119*

2. M. Griaule — *Conversation* with Ogotemmeli. London, OUP for IAI, 1951. (Revised Edition, 1965), p. 11

3. O.U. Kalu — Precarious Vision: Africa's perception of his world. In O.U. Kalu (Ed)) *Readings in African Humanities: Africa's Cultural Developments*. Enugu-Nigeria: Fourth Dimension Publishers, 1978. p 39

4. E. E. Evans-Prichard — Nuer Time Reckoning. *Africa*. Vo. X1 (1939), p. 190

5. M. Eliade — *The Myth of Eternal Return*. (Princeton, NJ. Princeton University Press, 1974, p. 18

6. J. S. Mbiti — *New Testament Eschatology in African Background*. London, SPCK, 1971. [/ 24 – 25

7. N.S. Booth Jr. — Time and Change in African Traditional Thought. *Journal of Religion in Africa*, Vol. 7/2, 1975, p. 82

8. Evans-Pritchard — Ibid, p. 202. See J. Bohanan, A Genealogical Charter. *African*, vol. 22, October 1952

9. Kalu — ibid; p. 40

10. Kalu — ibid. p. 41

11. Kalu — ibid; p. 41

12. T.O. Ranger — The Churches, the Nationalist State and African Religion. In Fashiole-Luke, et al. (eds), *Christianity in Independent Africa*. (Ibadan Nigeria, Ibadan University Press, 1978), p. 492

13. Robin Horton — Cited by Ranger, p. 492

14. M. Wilson,   *Religion and Transformation of Society*. (Cambridge, CUP, 1971, p. 18

15. M. Wilson,   ibid; p 106

16. E. Ilogu   The problem of Christian Ethics among the Igbo of Nigeria. *Ikenga*, Vo. 3/1& 2, 1975), p. 43

17. F. Arinze   *Sacrifice in Igbo Religion*. Ibadan Nigeria, IUP, 1970,p.31

18. J. V. Taylor   The Primal Vision. (London: SCM Press, 1963) p. 63

19. J.S. Mbiti   African Concepts of Sin. Frontier, 7/1, (1964) p. 18

20. Chinua Achebe   The Problem with Nigeria. (Enugu-Nigeria, Fourth Dimension Publishers, 1983)

CHAPTER SIX
Further Implications of Beliefs and Practices for Development

Introduction

Religion is not a philosophical or an intellectual assent to a form of creeds. Rituals, which are usually practical demonstration of beliefs, have far reaching socio-economic implications for the development of human society. People's beliefs affect their actions in one way or the other although some actions may not have a systematically set out intellectual explanations. For the Africans who see the world in a holistic perspective, one form of thought pattern affects a lot of other things in life. The rituals express the innate desires of the participants and celebrants. The goal is to bring the *unconscious* to the realm of *consciousness and reality*.

In small scale preliterate African societies, rituals stood out as dominant elements of religion .One of the continuing needs in any society is an appropriate imagery through which human beings can achieve some measure of consciousness. Thus, in traditional African communities, ritual celebrations became occasions for consolidation of group solidarity and integration of a person or a group of persons into the larger social system. In both local and wider spheres of interaction, Africans look for symbols, which commend group solidarity. Rituals, beside other functions, reconcile conflicting parties. In addition, they serve as security and guarantee of assurance of support from Divine Beings, who are the recipients of the ritual offerings.

The efficacy of rituals springs from the fact that, the rituals themselves represent eternal realities- *birth*, *maturity*, *marriage*, *family consecration*, *initiation into several secret and open societies*, *death*, *etc.* The problem is that in a period of rapid social change, there is the tendency for a people to forget the meaning and significance of traditional symbols even when old forms of the act are maintained. This raises another problem- *that of relevance.* How can a particular symbol or ritual be helpful and *functionally expedient to every generation?* It is in the light of this that some traditional rituals, which existed in the distant past and in some other forms still in many places, can be seen today as integral part of the community. They do not act as facilitators or motivators to socio-economic or cultural development of the people per se but as marks of identity and social cohesion. Those who enacted the rituals had the interest of the community at heart but with passage of time, their actions turned to act on the contrary. In other words, some of the rituals turned to act *as obstacles to the welfare of both the society and the individuals in it.* A few examples of such rituals would be analysed here to validate this point. The functionality and values of any traditional ritual should be seen within its own context It can also be analysed within the context of wider changing community since what happens in one small scale community may affect a large number of people in different places within a very short time.

We intend to look at rituals in *relational* rather than *timeless (eternal) perspective.* In other words, what apparently served some useful purposes or met the needs of a particular generation might turn out to be against the aspirations and needs of another. In a world of rapid social change, functional values of any institution or object must be given a very serious critical examination. This will place any action or thought within the scrutiny of its values in the life of a wider society. If functions and meanings of any ritual are not in line with people's needs, no sane group should try to perpetuate it simply *because it is a part of the tradition of the ancestors.*

6.1   Human Sacrifice and Ritual Killing in African Societies.

We had earlier mentioned this briefly in connection with African world-view and concept of time. African belief is *Life-Affirming* as well as *World-Affirming.* Yet, there are certain rituals which degrade and contradict the dignity and sacredness of the individual person and evidently dehumanised the individual person and life. Human sacrifice practised in many societies was based on the principle of the *Pre-eminence of the Life of the Society* rather than that of an individual. The individual comes and goes but the society remains eternally. This presumably was what Emile Durkheim meant when he stated that the *Deity, which people worship, is the Society itself.* Human sacrifice may not be peculiar to African traditional societies but was common in many *primary and non-industrialized societies.*

It takes different shapes in contemporary times. For instance, Capital Punishment could be seen as a form of getting rid of the life of a criminal or anti-social person in the community for the good of the wider society. The Jews who practised this form of punishment might have copied it from the pagan neighbours. Similarly true worship of Yahweh did not allow the use of human sacrifice as a form of rituals to the God of the Hebrews. The *Leviticus Laws* strongly condemned it. God's provision of a substitute ram when Abraham wanted to sacrifice his only son Isaac was a strong reference term to the Hebrews that Yahweh hates human sacrifice. Some traditional and tribal societies did not only perform human sacrifice but also practised cannibalism- either as a way to show strength or as alternative supply of animal protein that was in short supply in primitive society.

What we call human rights in our own time was either non-existent or grossly suppressed in traditional African world. Incidentally, the gross abuse of human rights, which is noticed in many African countries today, is a grim reflection of the ancient and long-standing tradition. An individual could be offered to a deity or used for the burial of a local Chieftain or King, and no one would question the right of the community to do so. Some leaders in Africa could detain or imprison an opposition leader in his community without reference to the rule of law. Protests by a few dissenting voices could be suppressed. In some cases fake charges might be levelled against the critics of the system and without giving them any fair hearing, they could be hanged. This is done in the pretext of defending the interest of the larger community. When it is presented as a way to defend the security of the larger community, many people, especially those who would not like to suffer similar fate, would not speak out in condemnation of the brutal act. Many of such abuses have gone unchallenged. This is the modern form of the sort of tyranny that prevailed in the past when individuals were offered to the gods with ease.

Those who offered fellow human beings to their gods either for the welfare of the entire community or because human life was considered the highest object that could be offered to a deity, undermined individual rights to life, self-expression and freedom. They invariably denied the community the opportunity of benefiting from such individual's gifts and talents that could have contributed to the growth and development of the wider community. The Kings, who were buried with a retinue of slaves, wives, etc, were thought to be Representative Personality- who stood for the Society itself. Some Kings were thought of as *Divine or Semi-Divine Personages*. In societies with such belief systems and rituals, human potentials could not be explored to the full. Life expectancy was short and unpredictable. A genius could be caught by a gang of ritual experts and be used for a barbaric sacrifice. Mobility and communication, which were essential for development, were badly restricted. Trade was badly affected since people could not risk long distance market enterprise without risking their lives. However in some cases, traders obtained passes for safe trip to another village market through their own leaders who provided them with guards and guides.

The evil of human sacrifice was one of the greatest problems that the colonial government and Christian Missionaries fought against in many parts of Africa. They were in the vanguard of the campaigns against practices like *killing of twin babies, trial by ordeal and human sacrifices- practices which the British administrative officers denounced as barbaric, but which formed part of the social and religious life of the community.*[1] Christian missionaries, in particular, were instrumental to the abolition of many obscene and sordid rituals. Aspects of the traditional government that were repugnant to the European and Christian ideas of what constituted good government, were vigorously challenged and fought against.[2] Although some of the practitioners of the rituals of human sacrifice in the past might have carried out the act out of genuine love the community and fear or love of the local deity, it led to gross abuses at certain periods in time.

Archdeacon Dandeson Crowther was particularly sad to observe that even some years after the Christian Missionary activities around Nembe (Brass) in the Delta Region of Southern Nigeria, some of the baptised chiefs had fallen back to the sordid practice *of human sacrifice, twin murders, customs which were considered sacred in traditional societies.*[3] The missionaries, under Bishop S. A. Crowther, and later his son, Archdeacon Dandeson Crowther, offered protection to those who were compelled to undergo **trial by ordeal** because such practices were based on superstition and were considered unjust to be carried out in any civilized and developed society. In 1885, for instance, Anderson, one of the Presbyterian missionaries in Calabar, gave asylum in Duke Town Mission House, to two men and a woman accused of causing the death of a little boy by *Ifot (preternatural powers of witchcraft)* and therefore were called upon to undergo trial by ordeal by the entire community. The new Consul, Mr Hutchinson, supported Anderson and both of them tried to enforce the law against human sacrifice.[4] Such hideous practices denied an individual a fair chance to look for redress when accused of any offence. The system of Trial by Ordeal denied any suspect the right to look for redress or the right o defend oneself.

It is not repetition of the obvious to state that until the advent of Christian missionaries and colonial administrators, the birth of twins was seen as a crime or taboo in many African societies. It is sad to note that the killing is still being practised secretly in many rural communities far from the eyes of law enforcement agents and Christian Churches. Many women were rendered childless, dehumanised or even killed for giving birth to twins. Some of the babies who were killed could presumably lived to become great leaders and experts in some fields of human endeavours in their various communities. Through such practices and rituals, society lost many of those who could have made their own contributions to the development of the world. Many children were thrown away into the sacred grooves and shrines because they cut the upper incisors first or arrived with both limbs instead of their heads. It was the strong traditional religious belief of the time that regarded such biological accidents or genetic mutations as crime against the deities and a pollution of the society. In a *precarious universe*, any aspect of abnormality was seen as a disruption of the order, which could spell doom to the living.

We are aware of the great achievements of some distinguished men and women who were born twins or with some deformity, but were rescued by Christian missionaries when the villagers threatened to kill them. Those who still justify the glorious African past, without qualifying it clearly, could have fallen victims to any of those practices, if they had lived in the so-*called old good days of African Age of Innocence.*

African intellectuals and true nationalists must be objective in their analysis of the past and come out with pragmatic answers to the perennial problem of *underdevelopment*. It is improper to continue to live with a system of thought and practices that abuse the rights of individuals, a system that encourages mismanagement of public funds, incessant ethnic wars and rivalry, gross abuse of offices at the detriment of the poor. A reflection on how to move ahead and not allow the old belief systems block the chances of moving up must be done. It is unfair to continue to work with principles and ideas that hinder people from moving on.

6.2   Caste System

There is no classless society but one of the most obnoxious, repressive and reactionary features of African societies, even in modern times, is the persistent existence of the *Caste System* in various forms in many ethnic groups. It is an ancient oppressive form of apartheid system, which the many parts of Africa do not understand. The Caste System in some African communities and ethnic groups resembles social stratification in biological concern with differences of birth and marriage.[5] It operates in such a way that people see it as an endogamous and hereditary subdivision of an ethnic unit occupying a position of inferior rank in comparison with other subdivision.[6] This is a very complex phenomenon and does not take a uniform shape in every part of African. One thing that is common in it, is that it reduces the status of an individual in the society to absolute nothing. In communities where a form of Caste System exits, it operates in its own peculiar way and excludes some people in the community from enjoying the full membership and participation in the affairs of the community. In its simplest form, this is what we mean by Caste Systems in Africa. Commenting on the meaning and implications of Castes, especially as it is practised in some parts of the Sub-Saharan Africa, David Sills stated that,

> *castes are special form of social classes which in tendency at least are present in every society. Castes differ from social classes, however, in that they have emerged into social consciousness to the point that custom and law attempt their rigid and permanent separation from one another.*[7]

It is important to state at this point that the discriminatory practice of caste system is not highly pronounced in all African societies, particularly in some of the areas examined by the present writer during the fieldwork. This does not mean that all citizens received adequate or similar attention and equal rights in the communities where the survey was carried out. It is still unfortunate that discrimination based on either gender, lineage, ethnic origin or social class is still prevalent in many societies. This discrimination is worse in communities who had *War-hero ancestors* who captured some people during the period of inter-tribal and inter-village wars in pre-colonial days. Some of the war captives settled and were made to serve as either slaves or domestic servants of the war-lords.

Others were sacrificed or dedicated to the patron deities of the clans as *cult-slaves*. It is this last group that would engage our attention in this analysis. Their descendants have suffered all sorts of discrimination in places where they live even in this modern time.

Initially, the *Cult-slaves* enjoyed a lot of immunity in the community because they were seen as *sacred and bona fide property of the deity, as a result of the dedication to serve the deity perpetually*. The community respected them for being the special servants of the gods. They were taken to be holy persons set apart for the services of the deity. The idea of sacredness had a connotation of separation from the ordinary and common persons and things. The idea has a subtle element of fear in primary societies that were basically *religious* and at the same time *superstitious*. The cult-slaves at that time were regarded as special religious functionaries and servants of the gods. The respect later degenerated first into fear of touching or tampering with the property of the deity and gradually ended up into discrimination. Whenever the deity needed human victims for ritual sacrifices, the children of the cult-slaves would be used for that purpose. They lived close to the shrines of the deities they were dedicated to serve or near to the market squares. This kept them a distance from the hamlets of the other members of the community for fear of being polluted by close contact. The *physical distance* between the homes of the cult-slaves and the residential quarters of the other members of the community gradually created a *social distance*. The cult-slaves began to suffer some social handicaps, kept out of *close touch* and interaction with the other members of the community. This is the background to the pejorative term **untouchable**, which people used to describe the cult-slaves in many places. The name became synonymous with lower social class, people of lower estate, cult slaves and non-indigenes of the community. With time, each generation widened the gap between them and the offspring of the cult-slaves and the social stigma placed on them became *institutionalised*. Hitherto, descendants of cult-slaves, up to five or six generations have suffered untold misfortune, discrimination, humiliation and denial of rights and privileges to rule and lead in the community. This background historical resume looks too simplistic but a ritual that began as a religious act two or four centuries ago in some places has kept many people into perpetual state of humiliation.

Among the Igbo of Nigeria, for instance, the type of Caste System that has persisted for about five centuries is the Osu System. From a wide field data

UDOBATA ONUNWA

collected by the present writer, the discrimination which this class of citizens has suffered is based on the fact that their ancestors were cult-slaves, war captives or slaves bought from slave dealers and offered to the deity. They therefore do not claim to be full members and indigenes of the community where they and their ancestors had lived for over four hundred years. Many of the living progeny of those early cult slaves cannot trace their origin to any other place in the world. An eminent Igbo anthropologist who vehemently deplored this ancient practice of discrimination explained that the

> *Osu (the Igbo outcaste), are people with status stigma people hated or despised yet indispensable in their ritual roles, people whose achievements are spurned by a society which are aggressively achievement-oriented.*[8]

It is unfortunate that the Igbo of Nigeria, known for their republican system of government and serious egalitarianism would continue to hold back some members of their community from achieving the highest level of respect and influence. Meanwhile, it has been confirmed from recent data that no one in Igbo society who belonged to the ancient Osu Caste performs the religious functions assigned to their ancestors. This is because people abandoned faith in some of the local gods and turned to Christianity. Besides, the law of the country does not allow any one to impose any religious function on any citizen. Yet, people have not stopped regarding the descendants of the Osu as outcastes.

Many people who descended from Osu ancestry have attained high status in modern social ranking based on Christianity, Western Education and wealth. They were among the earliest people to receive Christianity and the western education, which came as part of Christian mission package. We have first, second and even third generation of high court judges, top medical practitioners, university academics, accountants, engineers and clergymen, successful business and commercial magnets, who are descendants of Osu ancestry in many communities. Unfortunately, many of the do not receive them due recognition and respect they deserve in the local communities they call their villages or town. In a subtle way, the wider community treat them with spite and do not allow them openly to take some honorific titles exclusively reserved for the descendants of those founding fathers of the village. There is strict prohibition of marriage between the *Osu* and the *Diala* (descendants of the founding fathers of the community) who claim to come from noble ancestry. It is usually regarded as taboo or humiliation for the Diala to enter such relationship, which meets with clan or family resistance. Christians are equally guilty of this institutionalised discrimination. At times fear of the visitation of the angry ancestors make people who claim to be Christians or enlightened shun such relationships and interaction.

Commenting on the awful nature of this Osu System among the Igbo of Nigeria, Mary Ellen Ezekiel, a few years ago, lamented that the Osu

> *are born beautiful, they are born gifted, they are the cream of the land, Judges, lawyers, beauty queens, academicians, and magnates. But they are also cursed. They came from a society where a man's achievements could earn him the highest traditional titles. But they cannot aspire to one. For they are born with a stigma, the stigma of Osu Caste System. Their iniquities are the iniquities of their fathers visited on the children, their sin is ancestral. Sins they are supposed to have committed years ago before Christianity gained roots in Africa, sins which set them apart, tagged them unclean and made them forever Untouchable generation after generation.*[9]

The discrimination against the so-called Osu people has been a source of annoyance and conflict in many communities particularly where many enlightened and highly placed citizens are discriminated against and denied positions of leadership because they descended from Osu Ancestry. It is an act of gross abuse of Human Rights and unpardonable injustice. Many of the so-called Osu are gifted men and women who are successful in their chosen careers and could use their gifts and skill for the development of their local communities as well as the country. Some of them who are kept off from playing public roles in public life in their local communities decided to invest their resources and skills in places outside their native homes and countries where they felt accepted and respected. Discrimination against the Osu, which is based on primitive superstition and fear, has robbed Africa and the Igbo in particular of the benefits from the contributions of gifted men and women who could have otherwise identified fully with the aspirations of their people.

The Caste System has done a lot of harm in communities where it exists and its practice has been institutionalised. An Igbo learned academic and Roman Catholic Prelate, Archbishop S.N. Ezeanya, had in the past mounted an enlightened programme on the menace of the enigma called the OSU System. He stated that the whole phenomenon originated from the traditional Igbo man's anxiety to satisfy the demands of the spirits for best possible victim.[10] This is another form of abuse of human rights because it is unjust for one to use another to satisfy the demands of an angry spirit. There many people in Africa now who are calling for total abolition of all forms of discrimination. It began a long time ago. Caste System is not only discriminatory but also inherently dehumanising and retrogressive.

According to Bilton,

> *slavery … draws most rigid legal boundaries between members of one class and another. In this system, some human beings are regarded as chattels or items of property belonging to another individual or society.*[11]

The Church has consistently taught people that Caste System is not only evil and unproductive but also unrewarding. The essential doctrine of the universal brotherhood of mankind had been propagated for long to encourage men and women to contribute their best to the development of society. The call for the abolition of any form of caste system in Africa has, however not made much impact on the people. The Government of the former of Eastern Nigeria passed a Bill in 1955 abolishing the Osu Caste System but this did not go far in integrating the different groups of people into one unit. The Church, on the other hand, felt much would not be achieved by sheer force but a change of heart through the enlightening power of the Holy Spirit. Here again, another Roman Catholic Prelate, Bishop M.O. Unegbu, picked up the gauntlet and spoke of the roles of Christianity in a problem like this, if people would allow the teaching of the Church to direct them on the need for peaceful and harmonious co-existence. He spoke of the noble roles of Christianity which

> *emphasise our common brotherhood, our noble dignity as human beings, our equal status as God's children especially by becoming man and dying for each man. Christ destroyed all distinctions. Dying, he destroyed death, rising he restored our life. After him, there is no more distinction between Jews and Gentiles, between circumcised and uncircumcised*[12]

Caste System has denied many young people the opportunity to marry the persons they loved, denied progressive and gifted men and women the privilege to serve as leaders and representatives of their communities at policy making bodies in their countries. It has hindered intimate social relations between one group and the other. It has destroyed mutual trust and inter-group relationship and fellowship. It is a reactionary and an unjust system, which has widened the gap between one group and the other. It is an abominable practice, which like the apartheid policy creates rancour, instability, disunity and suspicion in society. Caste system was founded on traditional religious beliefs and has invariably increased the rate of *social, economic and political underdevelopment.* Any system which denies equal opportunity to all people, in un-progressive and would never build a solid and lasting democracy necessary for development.

6.3   The Cult of Secrecy and Reticence

One of the devastating characteristics of African Religion and Culture is its irresistible desire to keep secrets or lock up itself in its own enclosure. In the first instance, it is not a Missionary Faith, and does not openly propagate its beliefs and practices to outsiders. Although it is good that the religion does not impose itself on any one, it has at the same time closed its doors to people who would have liked to learn some of its tenets or borrowed some of them. Many Africans have been influenced immensely by this very inward-looking characteristic- the desire to keep every knowledge secret from other people.

A typical votary of African religion likes to hide facts of his faith and achievement from others especially one who does not understand the local language. This might be one of the problems of the early field workers who went to Africa for research. As a non-classical society, most scientific discoveries and repositories of wisdom and knowledge were not preserved in written forms. The African wisdom is not written down in books but in the hearts of the votaries.

As indicated already, one of the elements of traditional religion and culture is the belief that power resided in certain substances created by God People can use such powers for the good of the society especially for treatment of diseases. It is well known that there are those who have the knowledge to manipulate these substances for both good and evil purposes. Medicines in Africa are used to secure power, restore health, fertility, personality or moral reform. They may be used to heal or deliberately destroy life too. There is no such a thing as chance effect in African traditional thought-pattern. Differences in fortune even in present-day Africa are attributed to possession of portent medicines and charms. We had discussed this in passing in Chapter Three.

Many people in Africa make new breakthroughs and discoveries regularly in the area of traditional medicine. The traditional healers still keep their techniques and materials as well as their discoveries out of reach of any other person, including their professional colleagues. There has been consistent call by Western-trained medical practitioners in Africa on indigenous traditional healers for integration of some valuable aspects of traditional medicine with Western medicine. They feel this would be in the best interest of the Africans who should benefit from the two systems of knowledge. Some governments have encouraged this type of sharing of knowledge for improvement of services. Unfortunately, the traditional healers are suspicious of the intentions of the governments and the Western-trained medical practitioners. There had been long misunderstanding between the indigenous healers and the Western- trained medical doctors who see the other as *quacks, magicians, impostors and occultist.* The greatest reason for the refusal lies in the fundamental bases on which traditional medical practitioner operate- the cult of secrecy. Thy do not allow an outsider to have access to their operational system, instruments and materials. Such would betray the source of power of a medicine man. He would never like to disclose the secrets of his success to others. He does not want a colleague to overtake him by borrowing from him. Some apprentice medicine men qualify from their masters' practice without knowing much until they begin on their own. At times the labels on good medicines given to a patient are removed, so that no one can decipher the formula the medicine man has used in preparing his concoctions. No traditional medicine man is prepared to disclose the materials or equipment he uses for achievement of his feat. Through this secret way of hiding facts and scientific knowledge, many gifted men and women had died without sharing their skills and knowledge with others. Through such selfish and secret way, many traditional scientific discoveries had died with their founders and discoverers. Africa has lost a lot through these narrow ideas of preservation of knowledge and wisdom. Many illiterate African great healers did not write down their discoveries and died with them.

Some good field researchers had encountered difficulties in trying to obtain information from many learned and wise elders in the villages. They are very reticent and niggardly of the information they divulge for fear that such would be used against their system. It is a fact of life that when knowledge is shared, it is multiplied and when constructive criticisms are made on any project, there is usually an improvement in the next.

We cannot retrieve the ancient wisdom of many African civilizations and cultures for two principal reasons. One was the problem of non-classical society where nothing was preserved in documented form. The greater difficultly was caused by the incurable habit of withholding information from people. Many Africans grew up with the ugly habit of keeping their work secret from others. Unfortunately, we have lost a lot of treasures because of bad habit of keeping useful information away from public knowledge. The joy of hiding the secrets of success, the pride of self-confidence and glory of being the only one who knew the secrets, are among the motivating factors, which make like-minded persons bind themselves into close-knit clubs, and societies where they share ideas and secret knowledge which they hide away from non-members and outsiders. Many of them within such clubs still keep some ideas secret from some category of members whom they do not consider capable or knowledgeable enough to be confided in.

Men in particular, like to organise themselves into such clubs that claim to *have esoteric powers and knowledge which other people who are not members of their society or fraternity do not possess.* This is one of reasons for joining Secret Societies in some African communities examined by the present writer. It was discovered that men who make them exclusive to themselves formed traditional Secret Societies. Some of them allow female members who do not rise very high in the Club's hierarchy and power structure. There are no Secret Societies exclusively for women. Although the desire to keep secrets of the wonders of the Spirit World is the motive for joining Secret Societies, Ogbu U. Kalu had else where outlined a number of other reasons which motivated men from South Eastern Nigeria to bind themselves into such clubs. Such according to him were meaningful in the traditional and rural communities where

> *sex and wealth differentiation, the power and wonder of the Spirit World, the mystery of secrecy and in some cases, political power...among the greatest attractions for people to join Secret Societies*[13]

One other awful dimension of the traits to hide facts and keep them secret from others is the practice of the obnoxious and inhuman *witchcraft and sorcery*. It is outside the scope of this study to argue whether witchcraft is real or not in Africa. That argument which had engaged anthropologists and missionary preachers for a long time is now an over-flogged issue. Suffice it to say that Africans believe that they suffer from the attack of witches and sorcerers. They believe that the spirits of both men and women living in this world of time and space can be manipulated and sent out of the body on errands to do havoc on other persons in body, mind or estate, and that witches have guilds or operate singly. The spirits sent out of the body in this manner for such diabolical mission, can act either visibly or through a lower creature, which can be an animal or a bird.[14] Whether imagined or real, the problem of witchcraft had been a serious one in many African societies and hitherto, many people fear members of the cult. It can be seen as a negative aspect of African Spirituality. The ability to contrive such tricks to deceive or terrorize people is amazing in itself, if it is proven to be a hoax. However, the ability to conceptualise and visualize is not denied the Africans. The practice of witchcraft is based on the basic belief that some individuals misuse their *psychic powers* for diabolical purposes. Such people could not direct their psyche to conceptualise higher inventions that could be profitable to the general public. They rather use such esoteric powers and knowledge for evil purposes. People claim to make *soul-travels and astral-travels* into space while in a trance. These are magic concepts, which are beyond the realm of empirical examination. During the period, they could commute to different parts of the universe (they want to visit as they claim) and transact any business they wanted. The African notion *of soul transmigration* is based on the same principle of *metempsychosis*. Unfortunately, the Africans do not use their own psychic powers to conceptualise the invention of heavy industrial machinery for agriculture, sophisticated equipment for research into healing and other areas of human needs.   The use of one's inherent secret powers for destruction is devilish, anti-social, inhuman and unproductive. Through the abuse of such God-given powers by those who possess them, some progressive young men in families and communities where witchcraft is practised, are *mysteriously harmed, killed or rendered invalid*. This is one of the most difficult aspects of the traditional cults and it is inexplicable to the *non-initiates*. Some votaries of the traditional religion and culture have consistently refused to explain the internal dynamics of the system to researchers especially those whose mission they suspect. The fear of witchcraft, whether it is real or imagined, has crippled the ability of people to explore and invent new things. People had been held in bondage for long. Many talents are therefore, hardly developed to the full.

The idea of witchcraft and secrecy gains currency in another dimension-that of sorcery. We have earlier in Chapter Three discussed the differences between the two phenomena. However, the concept of sorcery is based on the principle that one can cast some spells from distance and cause harm on another object or another person. A person can use *magical* charms to influence another person, system or object and cause harm from a distance without necessarily going there physically. The ability to tap the mystical powers in nature could be used for both good and evil purposes. More often than not, the ability is hidden from people and those who *possess it or claim to possess the power use if for selfish and devilish ends.*

Africans waste a good deal of human and natural resources in an attempt to preserve the *cult of secrecy and reticence.* Those who operate at that level still find it difficult to open up and share their gifts and wealth of knowledge with others. Consequently, valuable treasures and resources are lost and people's progress and development hindered.

6.4   Taboos and Totems

Every society has got its checks and balances built into its cultural system to keep rebellion-prone humans from disrupting the social order. Humans must be made to conform to a particular pattern of life and order so that the social system remains constant. Such harmonious order would enhance creativity, productivity and invention needed for progress and development. No progress, good ideas and inventions can come or thrive in a confused and disorganised environment. Enforcement of societal discipline could be achieved through enactment of laws and rules of life to guide all inhabitants of a given community. Taboos are therefore, a part of the *social constructs* devised by a society or its elders and thinkers, for preservation of the environment and living creatures in it. It is self-imposed. Religion gives validation and authenticity to such *constructs*. In other words, through religious beliefs and practices, myths of origin could be formulated to give taboos and totems some marks of antiquity and originality. Totems are animals that a society decided *to deity* in a ritual ceremony, which marks a beginning of the worship or reverence of such animals as important religious objects in the social and religious history of the community. One ceremony of *deification* may have long term socio-religious influence on the life and outlook of the community in relation to that totem, which they have set up for themselves and generations yet unborn. Through religious rituals, a ceremony of deification of an animal becomes incorporated into the history of a community. Myths and legends, stories and sacred tales would be invented to validate the act of inauguration. From that day, members of the community and sojourners in their midst would be forbidden from killing, harming, maiming let alone eating an animal that has been so deified and made into a totem. Some totems receive offerings in the community and people offer sacrifice to them as a mark of loyalty. Unfortunately, many of the taboos and totems have got negative and inhibiting effect on persons and community in general. They thus become sources of danger and setback in the lives of the society.

It is easy to idealise the past and sigh for an imaginary *golden age* away from the disturbing present with its rapacious commerce, oppressive politics and bitter warfare. The facts are that in the past, there had been unpleasant customs and traditions, tyrannical leaders, sudden death, human sacrifice and other evils that were grossly disliked by the people, who, however, felt helpless to a very great extent to look for a way of escape. Although oracles and magic worked in favour of some people, they could work against others who paid less.[15] Totems which many communities worshipped or revered were animals which were believed to have got some historical or mythical connection with either the *founding fathers* of the community in prehistoric times. Each community had its own story of how its own totem animal came into being. A community inadvertently elevated the position of a totem into that of a deity. Such animals became permanent sacred figures that received worship and reverence. This is one of the reasons the early anthropologists described African traditional religions as *animism*.

Many repressive taboos were imposed on people to protect the sanctity of lives of the totems. Women and children became victims of those repressive laws and rules. This was common in many patriarchal societies. Many women and children lived below their rights and in most cases could not develop their talents to the full. Some naturally gifted women who could have contributed immensely to the development of the society , had they been given the opportunity, were handicapped by the oppressive taboos of the community devised by crafty and timid men to hold powerful and intelligent women in check. Children and women were in some communities denied some delicious meals and nourishing food items. The elders did this to stop them from greed and gluttony. Fro instance, women and young children were not allowed to eat eggs and meat so that they would not be tempted to steal when no one was around to check them.

Today, with the on-going struggle for the liberation of women from the crude dehumanising prejudices and torture of the past, many of them have come to occupy key and important positions in government, industry and other places of honour and responsibility in public life. The profile is rising. For instance we have many African women who are now serving as engineers, diplomats, architects, accountants, top university lecturers, high court judges, doctors, bankers and teachers, etc.

Taboos and totems held a greater part of the population in bondage. For instance, some of the totem animals that could have served as rich sources of protein in a community that lacked the basic nourishing food items and where malnutrition is taking its toll on the population are rather fed with eggs, chickens and other objects of ritual offerings. Big snakes or pythons are totems in some communities. Some groves and Sacred bushes which serve as shrines of divinities serve as homes of some of the totem animals. The land remains uncultivated. The good trees in them are not used for building projects. No one exploits the mineral deposits in those uncultivated portions on land. No one makes use of the reserves in those forests in communities where hunger is still a threat to lives of many.

It is sad to state that some of the traditional beliefs and practices constitute a barrier to the development of a good standard of living for the people. There are reports that many young people have fallen victims to crocodiles and wild animals that are totems in some communities. It is absurd and irrational in the light of present needs of modern society for a community to continue to provide food for some reptiles when their own children are hungry and malnourished.

Furthermore, in small-scale societies, a person's self consciousness is largely confined to the arts- myths, story telling, songs, sculpture and painting.

With modern man has come the flowering of science, the story of the universe and man's relationship with man through physical, biological and social sciences. Our knowledge of man in society has lagged behind our knowledge of the physical structure of the universe, perhaps because it is far more complex and perhaps we have been more fearful to study it.[16] It is not only fear of studying it, but also lack of the facilities to embark on such ambitions into the nature of the universe or into the unknown. Children, for instance, were not encouraged to ask questions or argue with adults because it would be a mark of rudeness to the elders. An adult would easily hush down a child who asks for detailed explanation for anything. The elders believed that a curious and inquisitive mind would not help a child to grow into a successful and reasonable man.

Nevertheless, there has been a great advance in the last hundred years or so in a person's knowledge of himself. The theory of evolution espoused by Charles Darwin, the conception of the Unconscious elaborated by Teilhard de Chardin, are landmarks in the process whereby humans are beginning to analyse themselves and their relationships with other people as well as to interpret themselves and their groups symbolically.[17] This breakthrough did not originate from Africa because of the pattern of thinking, philosophy and cosmology, under pinned by traditional religion and culture, which lacks the power for that. Not much along this line has been going on in Africa as of now, but something is about to begin in a large scale very soon. That will be along the line of self-consciousness when Africans will start to look both inwardly and outwardly for the reasons and answers to their problems.

NOTES

1. A. E. Afigbo   *The Warrant Chiefs*. London, Longmans, 1972, p. 73
2. A.E. Afigbo   ibid. ,p. 82
3. J.F. Ade Ajayi   *Christian Mission in Nigeria 1841 – 1892: The Making of a New Elite*. London, Longman, 1965, p. 226
4. J.F. Ade Ajayi   ibid; p. 119

5. H. H. Berton — *Encyclopaedia Britannica* vol. 12. New York, 1974, pp 983 – 990

6. David Sills (ed.) — *Encyclopaedia of Social Sciences.* Vol. 33&4, London, Macmillan, 1935.

7. David Sills (ed) — ibid

8. V.C. Uchendu — *The Igbo of Southeastern* Nigeria. New York, Holt, Reinhardt and Winston, 1965, p. 89

9. Mary E. Ezekiel — Osu- the Untouchable of Igbo Caste System. *Sunday Concord* Nigerian Weekly Magazine, Lagos Nigeria, 12 June 1983, p. 1

10. S.N. Ezeanya — The Osu (cult slave) System in Igboland. *Journal of Religion in Africa*, Vol. 2/2, 1968- 1969), p. 36

11. Tony Bilton, et.al. — *Introduction to Sociology.* London, Macmillan Press, 1981, p. 48

12. M.O. Unegbu — The Osu-Diala Scandal. *Lenten Pastoral.* Owerri-Nigeria, Assumpta Press, 1981, p. 3

13. O.U. Kalu — Missionaries, Colonial Government and Secret Societies in South-Eastern Igboland, 1920 – 1950. *Journal of Historical Society of Nigeria.* Vol. 9/1, 1977, p. 82

14. E.B. Idowu — *African Traditional Religion: A Definition.* London, SCM, 1973, p. 175 – 176

15. E.G. Parrinder — *Africa's Three Religions.* London, Sheldon Press, 1976, p. 90

16. Monica Wilson — *Religion and Transformation of Society.* Cambridge, CUP, 1971,p 131

17. Monica Wilson — ibid, p. 131

CHAPTER SEVEN
Christianity, Progress and Development in Africa

Introduction

This is not intended to be an advocacy for Christianity. It is rather an historical evaluation of some of the contributions of Christianity to the development of Africa. It does not gloss over some abuses carried out by some individuals who professed to be Christians or who probably claimed to be acting on behalf of Christian organisations or churches. More often than not, one error by an unenlightened individual can embarrass an organisation or a system. In other words, some errors committed by individuals in the exercise of their duty at a point in time should not be used to assess the ethos of an institution or organisation. This is therefore, an existential and objective evaluation of what Christian belief, teaching and practice can contribute to the development of a society. With respect to other World Religions, we must examine some valuable institutions and developments that grew out of the solid foundation of Christian history and ethics.

More often than not, it is easy to ignore the fact that some ancient civilizations had existed in different parts of the world. Many of them existed for some centuries before they declined and eventually disappeared. Their legacies are now past histories. Many industrialized and developed countries of the modern world had at a point in time benefited from the civilizing influence of Christian philosophy, ethics and doctrine. A few people in Europe and America may not believe that they are living on the civilisation that stands on the solid foundation of Christian enlightenment. The legal systems and to a large extent, the ethics and mindset, stand on the foundations of Christian teaching. It is the contention of this work that what Christianity did in the history of development and transformation of modern Europe and America, can also be experienced in Africa at some point in time.

Christian Characteristics

Christianity is a revolutionary and progressive faith. It is not the traditional religion of any people. No community claims it as its indigenous and natural religion. It is not a *national cult*. History has shown that Christianity contends with any religious or cultural system in a society it finds itself. For instance, in Palestine, the Jews did not want it to exist because it challenged their traditional and indigenous Judaism. They saw it as a travesty of their faith and a radical upstart that should be eliminated. When they discovered that Christianity was not a sect of Judaism, the zealous Jews began to persecute the few believers in Christianity ruthlessly.

The Roman Empire unconsciously provided the facilities and served as the *nursery bed* in which the young church was nurtured. The Imperial Government showed tolerance to any religious system in the empire on condition that the religion did not cause any breach of the peace. Thus the Imperial **Pax Romana** provided the peaceful environment and stable legal and social system that allowed the young Church to develop and expand through out the region. When the government wrongly suspected Christianity as a **state within a state,** Christianity suffered terribly in the hands of the emperors and their governors. They denied the Christians the usual freedom of worship and protection offered to other religions in the empire. Christianity struggled through the prevailing paganisms in many countries of Europe before it was able to establish itself.

The nature of Christianity automatically presents it as a challenge to any existing religious culture in any community it finds itself. It is a **transcendental and incarnate** religion that is also catholic (universal). Its universal nature is maintained in a special way- that is by being **supra- culture.** It transcends all human cultures, yet expresses itself through the culture of any local community it finds itself. In other words, Christianity does not show any special preference to any culture. This does not mean that it accepts every aspect of culture that is not helpful and edifying. It rejects any aspect of culture that it considers *retrogressive, oppressive* and *dehumanising,* however much the owners of that particular culture cherish it. Generally, Christianity does a lot of things to any culture it meets. First it absorbs its positive and progressive aspects, refines, purifies and expresses itself through them. Finally, it throws away what it considers obstacles to human development, progress and fulfilment inherent in that cultural system. This is exactly what Christianity did to the traditional cultural systems of the countries of Europe when it entered there. The cleansing and edifying power of Christianity in turn transformed those countries. It is wrong to say that Christianity is a European Religion. In historical fact, it is older in African than it is in Europe and America. The problem was that the original Christianity that entered Africa in first century of its existence did not take strong roots before militant Islam swept it off in the 6th Century. The form that later entered Africa in the 18th century wore the garb of European Culture with which it had clothed itself during the years of settlement and rehabilitation. Just as it passed through European cultures, *absorbed* them, *refined, transcended and expressed* itself through them, so must Christianity do to African culture if Africa must grow and develop. It must expunge the detestable elements that in its opinion are instruments of darkness, underdevelopment and oppression in Africa. This is the aspect of Christianity that makes it look revolutionary and leads it to frontal attack on any culture it meets. When it is fully absorbed into any cultural system, Christianity puts on the garb of that culture, speaks the language of the people and expresses itself through it. This is an aspect of its **incarnate** nature that confuses people and its detractors have capitalised on it to accuse Christianity of what it is not. For instance, in *Incarnation,* Jesus did not appear to humans as **pure, unrefined Word** but as **Word Incarnate**. This was to make himself easily understandable by humans and besides he used it as a means to identify with humanity in general. He speaks to any society in the language they understand and through their valuable symbols. This is the basis of the Kenosis Theology or the current concept of **Inculturation** which has been grossly misinterpreted in many quarters. We must understand that Jesus is the Lord of the Universe and that his Church is universal (catholic). It is only Jesus that is universal in absolute *sense.* The confession people make of him, their experiences of him and their expressions of their faith in him are factors of the variables of culture, language, temperament and ecology. This is fully expressed in the Pentecost event where *everyone present understood the very essential elements of salvation in his own mother tongue.*[1] People were surprised to learn that in spite of obvious human differences, every body understood each other without losing his own identity and authentic personality. The differences of race, nationality, status, culture and language did not hinder the expression of the essentials of the Universal Lord of the World. Each group related to God vertically and to fellow humans horizontally without any conscious efforts. Since Christianity cannot afford to stand outside human cultures, it permeates them, absorbs, purifies and propagates itself through them without preference to any.[2] If Christianity could not afford to limit itself or remain within Jewish cultures, it cannot afford to do so with European culture without extending to African and to other cultures.

There are several obstacles that restrict the absorption of Christianity into a cultural system. These among others include

i.   religious traditions, e.g. customs, ancestor cults

ii.   economic circumstances- economic dependency, exploitation, excessive acquisitiveness, etc

iii.   social ties, e.g. membership of secret cults, families, class

iv.   political sanctions e.g. anti-Church decrees, laws of Blasphemy etc

v.   ideological factors and world views, other value systems, group norms

vi.   types of thinking, concrete, abstract, impulsive.[3]

Some of the above conditions have made conversions difficult. For instance the fourth factor has been in operation in countries which impose religious laws on the citizens by making *State Religion* a compulsory thing. In that case, there is no freedom of worship and expression of faith. The fifth factor worked in many African societies. They make Christianity operate at the periphery of the community's life and this does not influence the people's life much. This is the cause of the differentiation of social class, level of development in different parts of the world. In any society where strong Christian foundation becomes the basis of growth and development, a radical transformation takes place. It stands the test of time. Such societies take the lead in the development of human intellect and natural resources. The citizens may forget this foundation and legacy after about four or five centuries but the fact remains that Christian traditions that had been fully internalised had placed the people on a vantage ground and it is difficult to uproot it.

7.1   Christianity and Development – a few examples from History of Nations

Although human society has passed through several phases in its development, it is important to glean a few concrete examples from the contributions Christian traditions had made in some parts of the world. In its various institutions, structural forms, manifestations in human society, Christianity has brought a lasting transforming influence that in a subtle way controls the modern world order. As an incarnate faith and a transcendental religion, Christianity makes claims on both the physical and divine aspects of human life. It is a *holistic faith* that takes care of *body, soul and spirit*. This view may sound dogmatic and could probably annoy some one who holds a different view. We need to turn to documented history dispassionately to assess the validity of some of these claims.

Christianity has acted as a custodian of human life and values. This is manifested by both Jesus and his immediate apostles who taught people that society should not be made a police state where rugged individualism and rape of human freedom take the place of cordial human relationships. Christian faith rejects despotism and anarchy that block the way to individual and corporate development and progress.

The purifying and humanizing impact of Christianity on the pagan and imperial vices of the Ancient Rome was tremendous. One needs not to be reminded of the outstanding position of the Church during the period of the *Dark Ages*. The Church stood like an institution of hope and harbour of light to the benighted humans of the age. No political philosophy or sociological principles, economic theory or religious system offered humanity the much needed light and guide during the era of intellectual darkness and frustration. The Church stood as the only source of inspiration and encouragement to the bewildered and confused human race. Besides, feudalism engulfed human society and enslaved it with its autocracy, wars after wars became obstacles to human progress and development. The Hundred Years War between England and France hampered meaningful human values and intellectual growth. It was the Church, more than any other institution that provided humanity with solace, succour and asylum from the weariness and trauma from the pressures of the period.

The Christian Church laid the foundation for the development of ethics and intellectual development of Medieval Europe. Both Rome and Constantinople, the two leading centres of learning in Western and Eastern Europe respectively produced intellectual studies that challenged and nourished the human mind. Other World Religions in the East, which tried to improve the spirit of man through mysticism left humans totally confused, blindfolded and disillusioned as well as underdeveloped. The religion that used warfare as a means of expansion and proselytising destroyed enormous structures that had been erected earlier. Modern world owes a lot to the Monasteries of the Mediaeval Europe. It was in those places that monks and clerics of different Orders in solemn contemplation propounded theories that helped the growth of modern science. The early modest beginning of Scholasticism- (the Universities of Bologna, Paris, Oxford and Cambridge) was entirely the responsibility of the Christian Church. No other religious system can challenge Christianity in providing lasting and globally copied civilization and development. Christianity provided the raw ingredients that ushered in the *Renaissance* that ultimately led to the dawn of the *Age of Reason*. This was the popular *Age of Enlightenment* in Europe. It is unfortunate that some brilliant brains developed the Spirit of Humanism that turned against Christianity after they had benefited from the opportunity it provided for education in science and philosophy. The Age of Humanism, no doubt challenged the Church to mend its fences and cleanse itself from any trace of despotism and pride that nearly derailed it from the path of rectitude and humane living. It is still amazing that the scepticism that thrived for a short period then affected only a handful of intellectuals. For the masses and a large number of intellectuals then, Christianity was the only and most meaningful part of existence. Secularisation only scratched at the periphery of human society. Humanistic philosophy did not provide theories that satisfied human minds, body and soul. Both Spinoza and Voltaire, who taught that the *Age of Reason* has come to give answers to all human problems, encouraged people to abandon Christianity. Both men could not escape the misery of shameful deaths!

Until the *Middle Ages*, Western Civilization was primarily a product of Christian teaching and direction. There was no specific challenge to Christian claims till the middle of 17th Century. The opposition of the *rationalists* did not stop the wheel of progress of the Christian truth from moving human society to the shore of progress, knowledge and development. Today, the leading industrialized nations of the West, (perhaps some may not believe it), owe their exalted position more to the Christian influence and teaching than to any other historical factor. They were not part of the erstwhile *Cradles of Civilization* of the Ancient World that crumbled after some time. The present richest and most developed countries of the world rose to their present prominent positions in a spectacular manner after the decline of many ancient civilizations that did not stand the test of time. Although anti-Church philosophy have come up in some of these countries at some points in time, the strong scientific foundation laid by Christianity had made immense contribution to the present growth and state of development.

It is still within the competence of documented history to state that progress in England through the *Industrial Revolution* operated within the teachings and influence of Christian ethics and doctrine. Max Weber's *Protestantism and the rise of Capitalism* goes far to confirm this fact. Christian education of human mind brought not only the forces that initiated industrial progress but also insisted that the revolution itself should put on a *human face*. Thus Christianity did not only prompt the factors that led to the *Industrial Revolution*, but also made the Revolution operate within the limits of human rights and serve human needs for the glory of God. Christian understanding and interpretation of human values provided the ethical principles that checked the industries from turning into centres of exploitation of the labours of children and women in the factories. Human values stood far above material profits. Christian ethics shaped Western attitude to work.

Christianity registered one of the greatest opposition against the Slave Trade. We still remember that the Anti- Slavery Movement had its origin in the Christian Evangelical Revival and Movements of the 19th Century in England. The Evangelicals understood the Biblical teaching on *freedom and salvation* proclaimed by Jesus Christ.[4] Sir Thomas F. Buxton, a leading Evangelical Christian in England, took up the campaign for the abolition of Salve Trade in a very serious way and rallied the support of like-minded people, both in government and in the Church. In his book, *The African Slave Trade and its Remedy*, Sir Buxton took up a commercial argument against the Slave Trade and converted it into anti-slavery slogan. Thus he insisted that

> *We must evaluate the mind of her (African) people and call forth the resources of her soil...Let the missionaries and school masters, the plough the spade go together and agriculture will flourish; the avenues to legitimate commerce will advance as natural effect, and Christianity operate as the proximate cause of this happy change.*[5]

Christian missionaries and many evangelicals in England rendered humanitarian services in Africa during their period of the campaign against Slave Trade. They made huge sacrifices in many ways. They knew Christianity as a force in transforming man's spiritual life as well as being a *civilizing agent* whose main aim is the improvement of human life both here and hereafter. Those early evangelicals had elaborate programmes for the improvement of Africa for the good of Africans. In their own modest way, they built up a programme in which:

> *The Africans protected by Britain, guide by the missionaries and working with capitals from European merchants, would not... stay shyly away from the people... but move inland and establish many factories at strategic points, living together in little colonies, little cells of civilization from which the light would radiate to the regions around. As catechists and school masters, they would preach Christianity, as carpenters, tailors, sawyers, masons, and artisans, they would improve the standards of housing and household furniture, and build necessary roads and bridges to make a highway for legitimate trade.*[6]

This comprehensive programme was seriously pursued by the Christian missionaries who made the government join them in the rehabilitation of the repatriated ex-slaves. From such humble beginnings, they helped to build such towns like Freetown in Sierra Leone and Monrovia in Liberia, both in the West African sub-region. Christian missionaries did all these at the expense of their lives. Many died for the sake of those they came to rescue.

Besides, there are strong evidences of the humanizing and progressive roles of Christian missionary activities in many developing countries of Africa, Asia and Latin America. In Ghana and Nigeria, for instance, the missionaries were seen by the local people as *purveyors of civilization and development.* Some traditional rulers and elders in the former Eastern Nigeria saw the missionaries and the faith they preached as agents and bearers of development. Rev Father Walker recorded the case of one Chief Idigo of Aguleri near Onitsha in Nigeria who invited the missionaries from their headquarters in Onitsha to come and open schools, hospitals and churches in his village like they had done in Onitsha. He saw the presence of missionaries in Onitsha as the cause of the progress and development in the area unlike in the surrounding villages where the missionaries had not entered.[7]

The chief of Nsugbe, another town close to Onitsha declared openly that he would become a Christian so that the missionaries would bring some *developments projects* in his town for his own people.[8] Although he had a wrong motive for being a Christian, he nonetheless, saw Christianity as a harbinger of the foundation on which people's life style is changed and improved for a higher standard. This was the popular view of many people of his generation and to some extent, they were right then. Hitherto, it is likely that some imbalance in educational development and progress in different parts of Africa can be traced to how the indigenous people received Christianity in the early years of mission enterprise in Africa. Those who rejected it and expelled the missionaries lagged behind in educational development, which hindered their people from making progress along the new ways of life and improvement of life expectancy. Those who rejected Christianity then are still complaining of being disadvantaged in several areas of life. They might be seen or considered as being developed in their own or along their own way of life but when compared in the index of world development and progress, they are still seen as *backward, primitive and underdeveloped.*

7.2   Christianity and Human Values in Africa

As an agent of development and *bearer of the light of progress*, Christianity has opened up many dark places in the world where its light has beamed on human society. It has improved individual and communal standard of living by challenging humans to bear one another's burden and to be their brother's keepers. We cannot discuss the development and civilisation of Western Europe without discussing the outstanding contributions of Christianity and its philosophy. Invariably, the history of the development of the modern Europe is that of the development of Christianity. Although they are two distinct institutions, they are inseparable in the sense that both had influenced each other in many diverse ways. Christian evangelisation of a place and people is synonymous with its development and enlightenment. Christian teaching and knowledge becomes a way of life as well as showing one the way to life.

We intend to examine some ways Christianity can assist in transforming and improving African societies with its positive and creative teaching and influence. Africa will change for better is she adopts and integrates the basic Christian principles to her way of thinking, living and doing things. Many sordid and hideous beliefs, despotic and tyrannical forms of leadership, which hinder individual and corporate development, will no longer plague a society that has truly incorporated Christian virtues in its ethical and moral laws. There are eternal truths in Christian teachings that transcend all cultures, temperaments and environments and if they worked in many other places, there is no doubt they would work in Africa.

Christianity in the Home

Christianity is interested in the welfare of the human family. As a faith that is out to offer humans total salvation, it touches every aspect of human life. It is not only in Africa but also in all human societies that Christianity has set out the ideal of family life. The Bible has outlined complete rules of life and ethical norms for the family. Whoever obeys those rules, despite his society will enjoy the bliss of God's blessings and promises. Those who ignored the basic principles of Christian family life ordained by God and enshrined in the Christian Scriptures despite nationality and religious belief, must continue to face domestic crisis that result from such lapses. Today, many families are facing all sorts of family problems because they often do not live in line with Biblical principles but have allowed the pressures of modern life to dictate and influence their way of life. This does not underestimate the weight of the pressure of modern and technological age. It is rather an affirmation that because the modern age is full of tension and frustration that one needs to depend on the eternal truth of the teachings of Christianity for guidance and protection in times of difficulty. The Bible, especially the New Testament is clear on the roles of each member of the family- parents, children, grand parents and other relatives.

There is no other religious system that has done more than Christianity in protecting the rights of women and children in the family. In Christianity, the legal and social rights of women and children are guaranteed without one fighting to obtain them. In traditional African societies as well as in other patriarchal societies, women were looked upon and treated like chattels of their husbands. The traditional societies and some religious customs and traditions held women down and did no allow them equal opportunities and rights with men. Christianity abrogated all inhibitions against women and elevated their status. It was Christianity that introduced women to school and helped them to study along side their male counterparts. Through such openings, intelligent and gifted women got the opportunity to improve their natural talents for the good of the entire society. Prejudice against women has denied the world many opportunities to benefit from the talents of many gifted women in the world. Many traditional laws against womanhood and particularly of widowhood and punitive as well as restrictive ritual laws imposed on women that kept them *perpetually in the kitchen* were removed by the teachings of Christianity especially when it entered some African villages. Women participate openly with men in the efforts at nation building in many countries especially where Christianity influenced their social and legal systems. A number of gifted women are now in top jobs as business executives, bank managers, diplomats, doctors, architects, engineers nurses, accountants, top legal luminaries, frontline politicians , etc because they were allowed to develop their intellectual ability without restriction. The opportunity to develop along this way was not there in all the countries of the world and had not been there since the world began. It has taken many years of persuasion and struggle to reach this level of human development. Christianity has been at the vanguard of the struggle for the elevation of humanity to God-given standard. Women in countries with strong Christian influence have excelled in career development more than their counterparts who live in countries with little or no Christian presence.

7.3   Christianity in Social Relationships

The grotesque and inhuman discrimination of people based on caste system is still practised in many parts of Africa. Discrimination based on whatever reason is found in every human society.

Any unscrupulous person can harbour the spirit of discrimination for whatever reason. Christian teaching is clear on the ways to relate to people and neighbours. In Christian principles of social relationship and justice, there is no barrier between Jews and Gentiles, black and white, rich and poor, male and female, slaves and freeborn, etc. This principle has broken all the man-made barriers that block inter-personal or any form of relationship in human society. Christianity has done a lot in creating the conducive atmosphere for cordial social relationships between persons and countries by preaching the powerful message of undying love. The current Human Rights laws against any form of discrimination have their roots in the principles of mutual love and justice which Christianity has been teaching and preaching for a long time.

Although some unscrupulous elements within the church may at times harbour some ill feelings against people from places other than theirs, Christian world-view makes one see the world as a global *village*. The question, who *is my neighbour?* has a Christian answer that transcends gender, nationality, culture, ethnic boundary, colour, religion, politics and status. The Christian faith has persistently encouraged humans to co-exist as people from one family and work towards peace. Many Charities that exist today practise ethical principles of Christianity to be one's brother's keeper and bear one another's burden. Humanitarian services carried out by men and women nurtured by the Christian faith down the centuries are still shining example of how to live in a world full of problems and hardship. The Bible has stood as an icon of light in condemning discrimination against any individual or group any time , anywhere even among its members. So it is normative Christian rule to see that all humans live like brothers and sisters in God-given society for the mutual benefit of the other to the ultimate glory of God.

7.4   Christianity in Economics and Politics

Although Christianity is not a game of politics and economics, it does not see them as evil but as important aspects of human activities that should be played to the rules for the good of society. Christianity affects every aspect of life of both the individual and society. It refines and directs life into the path of rectitude and productivity. We have earlier mentioned Sir Thomas F. Buxton's idea of *the Bible and the Plough*. It is necessary again to add a few things on how Christianity has helped in many ways to shape the lives of people in many other parts of the world and apply it to the African situation.

There are enormous human and natural resources in Africa. There is abundant investment potential in many parts of Africa. With honesty, integrity and resourcefulness, people can harness Africa's rich natural resources and build strong economy that can sustain growth and development. Leaders can build solid economy that can sustain a high standard of living for the people. Dishonesty and corruption among the leadership of many African nations have scared genuine foreign investors. The rich mineral resources are not tapped for the good of the entire nation and its people. If men and women of integrity would handle and manage Africa's rich resources, poverty and hunger would disappear. Political instability would give way to peaceful co-existence of people.

The traditional religious ethics that does not condemn a man who steals public funds and property and brings it back to his village has been one of the weak foundations on which African countries stand. Christianity condemns stealing or misappropriation of public funds and dishonesty in its entirety no matter who is involved. But in many African societies, public office holders who steal public funds to help their relatives and friends are not necessarily condemned by those favoured by the abuse of office and position. Often some communities honour their sons and daughters who used their public office to enrich themselves and their tiny villages and relatives. The African microcosm is the village setting and the other parts the country are seen as not a part of the person's world. A strong Christian teaching and moral education will enlarge people's scope and change their hearts to see the true meaning of *statesmanship* and nationalism.

The Church can help the countries build up this new moral life-style. A good Christian foundation needs to be laid and built upon if the nation is going to move forward. A new Christian orientation is important. The church can do this in several ways. We already discussed the principles of *The Bible and Plough* of T.F. Buxton. The Church in a particular village or zone can start a small fellowship group whose primary aim is to study the bible and apply its teaching to practical ways of life. One of those ways could be establishment of small co-operative shops or farms that can support local communities to earn a living. In some agricultural communities, for example, the Church can set up agro-based cottage industries which can offer employment to young people and women. They can produce food and sell to the community at cheap rate. The main capital take off can be provided by the Diocese or local government agencies or funds from any International Development Agency. The early missionaries in some parts of Africa introduced similar scheme which produced not only well trained and self-reliant honest men and women but also produced enough local food for the people. The two main problems here are the funds and the motivation. If the Church can provide the initial take off capital and resource people to train the local people on the methods, life will improve at the grassroots.

The Church in the past pioneered the establishment of craft centres, where pottery, carpentry, painting, tailoring and weaving were taught. The carpenters and bricklayers trained by the Christian missionaries in some *Christian Villages* and *Skill Acquisition Centres* established by the Church in the early 20th century turned out to be successful and progressive in their chosen trades. Some of them became wealthy men who established large industries that employed many young school leavers. One of those companies still exists in Benin Nigeria where the proprietor was a mission-trained skilled man who in turn began to train young people in his factory. If industries of such types are established today by the Churches, they would help reduce gross unemployment of many school leavers, check migration from the rural to urban centres and enhance the standard of living of many. Although several government agencies in Africa look serious in their determination to establish programmes that will create jobs for their young people, the Church had done so in the past and can continue to do so today to support what is going on in some places at the moment.

When people of proven integrity and accountability are in positions of trust, there is hope that conditions in the industries would improve. Most industries in Africa operate at loss because of a number of factors including incompetence and dishonesty. Some ambitious economic projects and financial institutions had suffered huge losses because of the management style of the people. If the basic economic principles are built on solid Christian ethics and protected with legal systems influenced by Christian sense of justice and fairness, they would stand any form of economic recession that people complain of in many African countries. When a system takes strong roots on Christian foundation, it would continue to grow even in a generation that may not profess serious Christian faith. Ethical principles built of solid Christian foundation stands the test of time.

In many African countries, between 80% and 90% of the population still live in the rural areas and practise subsistence farming. Economic development in the colonial and postcolonial period took two different forms in different parts of Africa. Everywhere, however, two outstanding models have been identified- either the activation or exploitation of unused natural resources-mining, exploration of mineral oil, or the transfer of resources out of subsistence agriculture into money earning activity. It is widely believed that not much happened in African economic life (in terms of money economy) until after the World War II.

The report of one International Bank in Nigeria, for instance, spoke of the leisurely pace of the pre-War economy. But the development before World War II was hardly leisurely either in Nigeria or in any other African country. Indeed, the rate of economic change and growth from 1900 – 1930 was relatively rapid in every sense. World War I slowed it somewhat and the depression of the late 1920s and early 1930s worsened the situation.[9] This does not mean that nothing happened in the distant past in this regard. Some economic contacts were established as already discussed in Chapter Two. But it was not elaborate and did not go far enough. Africans did not play a leading role or prominent roles in the business partnerships where they were established. Except in North Africa that was for long deeply involved in the lucrative trade

UDOBATA ONUNWA

with the East and parts of Central Europe, the other parts of Africa lived near monetary economic isolation from the outside world till of late. Even North Africa did not go far into Western Europe where Christian ethics shaped economic principles. She was instead deeply involved with the East where economic ways of life depended on other religious dogma and principles. Africa South of Sahara had only four points of contact with the outside world till as late as 1880. The four points were the ancient trans-Saharan trade between the Western Sudan and North Africa; Arab Settlements on the East Coast; the European trading posts on the West Coast of Africa and the European settlements on the Southern tip of Africa.[10] Goods and ideas had trickled into Africa through these routes for hundreds of years, but they had little impact on the lives of many who lived in the hinterland. South Africa had moved farther away in the direction of intensified contact than other areas, although before diamond was discovered in 1869, it was not much different from the rest of Africa.[11]

West Africa with its ancient trans-Saharan trade in some ways had a more intensive experience in money economy than had South Africa. Important commercial centres like Fez and Kano had flourished and impressed many explorers and merchants from Europe in the early 18th Century. Some business links did not last probably because of the link with Muslim Arabs whose own ways of life did not spread fast to attract the egalitarian traders in the hinterland. The West African Slave Trade led to the development of active money-oriented sectors e.g. in the towns like Whydah in Dahomey (Benin Republic) and Lagos in Nigeria. But European dealings with Africa for more than three hundred years were based mainly on slaves and did not require European movement into the hinterland. They failed to register any valuable and durable fundamental transformation in African Societies in terms of money economy because the trade was illegal and anti-social.

With the extension of scale and geometric growth in African population, it is difficult to depend on the traditional subsistence mode of farming and crude oil industry as the major source of economic maintenance. Cultural and social factors obstruct agricultural change and growth. Under traditional laws and norms land is held *commensally and in unconsolidated pieces*. This pattern of holding and inheritance reduced incentives to improve land and more importantly lack of clear cut ownership claims exposed land titles to uncertainty and made it difficult to establish systems of agricultural credits. We are also aware of the *sacred nature of the land* in many African societies. A deity highly revered in many societies governs the earth. The deity is the Earth Goddess generally believed to be a female deity in many communities, although the present writer discovered one of two communities that regard her as a *Male Deity*. The system of deification put many people off its use and the natural resources embedded in it. This happens where some portion of land is reserved as a grove or sacred shrine of the deity. Humans are therefore denied the full use of the land in many places on account of religious belief.

Christianity with its attendant form of enlightenment offers Africans opportunities of new patterns of land acquisition and utilization for the good of the general public. The so-called communal land where it exists is dedicated to a deity as a sacred grove or shrine. It remains uncultivated and resources in it untapped. People suspect that *demons and other spirits* live in such sacred forests. Large scale mechanized farming and irrigation cannot be embarked upon in many places because of the methods of land ownership and atomistic societies that have their own local native laws and customs. A lot of tribal chieftains have resisted efforts by some organisations to embark on a massive clearance of some extensive forests regarded as *sacred shrines* of the gods. The wide use of mechanization in agriculture is a product of industrialization that was influenced by Christianity. Improved tools of agriculture and accelerated research in the preservation of agricultural produce had led to food production in large and commercial quantities in many places in the recent past. Unfortunately, many people including the national governments ignored agriculture and focussed on mineral exploration as a way to build up the economy. The function of the Church is to lead, initiate new programmes and projects that can lead to improvement of living standard. The establishment of new institutions of education of children and adults, for the care of the sick, the aged, the destitute or for the fostering of skills and organising the people that they might feed themselves had been an integral part of the Church's ministry. This was evident in the Mediaeval Europe.[12]

Many unnecessary and wasteful socio-religious gatherings and jamborees common in the traditional African societies led to gluttony, drunkenness, avarice and immoral sex orgies. They usually happen during the many festivals that took place in many communities. Christianity moderates human life and directs how to live without people getting into such reckless way of life. In the industrialized parts of the world where Christianity is practised, such immoral things exist as a deviation from the norms of life but extravagant spending especially during funerals, is an unexpected way to show wealth, respect, and to the dead, and hospitality to sympathizers in many African communities. Christian work ethic which we had earlier discussed help a people's economic life style and can enhance the standard of living. If it is applied in Africa, there is hope that it would bring success and prosperity to individuals and communities.

7.5   Christianity, Patriotism and Nationalism

It is genuine love for God that breeds true love for the Fatherland. It is one who loves one's own country that can truly and correctly be described as a *patriot, statesman, a true citizen and a nationalist.* More often than not, people who claim to be patriotic hide some secret objectives in their hearts. We have seen many people who make much noise about justice and human rights when they are not in power or close to those who hold power. When some of them come to power, either by popular vote or through the barrel of the gun, they turn worse oppressors of the poor. A citizen who would not betray the secrets of his country, no matter the pressure on him to do so, can be seen as a patriot. A good citizen is a person who would not abuse any position of trust reposed on him by the people. A person who does not and would not take advantage of his or her position for personal gains at the expense of his country can be described as an honest citizen. These qualities are well established in many developed nations of the world. It is still not fully understood in many African countries and by many Africans. It is just the concept of democracy. The Western understanding and practice of it, is quite different from the way Africans do. The terms *patriot* or *nationalist* have been misused many times by too many social climbers and opportunists. Any true Christian is a patriot, always ready to die for the good of his fatherland, always ready to serve the country, always willing to do anything that will not bring disgrace to his country. A true Christian must serve his people and nation with love and commitment. A true Christian must pray for the leaders of his country, however bad they might be. A true Christian is always ready to criticise in love any aspect of life in his country that does not stand for justice and fairness. A true patriot is not one who winks at his nation's evils and hopes that all will be well when he knows that natural and divine laws are flouted without fear.

Love for one's fatherland can be shown in many ways. A prophetic self-criticism is one of the ways provided the critic does not go back secretly to do worse things. For instance the Old Testament Biblical prophets showed great love to their country by their consistent calls to the nation to depart from the ways that would bring destruction. They consistently warned the nation to desist from moral and religious lifestyle that encouraged gross injustice and social ills against the citizenry. Often their calls to the nation to depart from decadent ways were seen as a mark of unpatriotic attitude to the national cause. Jesus called his countrymen and women to retrace their ways of life and seek God's divine glory. He even wept for the impending doom he saw the nation was racing into. As a patriot, he did not hide his open criticism of the entire social system and prayed for them to seek God's light and truth and live. Eventually, Jerusalem was destroyed in AD 70 just as the Jews of the Old Testament times were carried into exile for not heeding the consistent calls of the prophets to rethink their ways.

Africa is poor today because of mismanagement of her resources. Some of the citizens of the African countries collude with foreign and multinational companies to defraud their own countries. Christianity teaches that one should not defraud at all, let alone one's own country or neighbouring country. Although Christianity is not a national religion, it teaches all citizens to respect the leaders and love their country. Besides, it enjoins all citizens to love their neighbours including other nations as well. In that sense, no one will seek the ill of the other nations around. Christianity has for long condemned all forms of dictatorship, tyranny, and authoritarianism. It has also denounced ethnic loyalty that can lead to bigotry to have and pillage other nations. One who loves and respects one's country will also respect the rights of the neighbouring countries. Human weakness has not allowed some patriotic leaders with strong Christian conviction to obey this rule totally.

To appreciate fully the role Christianity has thus far played in the development of modern Africa, it would be appropriate to look back at some of the processes that took place many years back. The influence of the Christian

Church on the minds and attitudes of some men and women who had played some roles in nation building can be seen against that background. Although things are not yet fully established and be the way they are supposed to be, we cannot say that many people had not made useful contribution based on the influence of Christianity on their life and faith. A few of the early *Pan-Africanists* in different parts of the continent during the heyday of colonial administration were ex-pupils of Christian Mission Schools and some even served as teachers or clergymen. Only four out of over three hundred languages in Africa had their *own native* scripts prior to the 18th and 19th Centuries when the missionaries arrived in Africa. Those four languages were the *Nsibidi*, which existed, in the Southeastern corner of Nigeria among the Igbo people. It was confined to the members of top traditional Secret Society called *Ekpe* who used it as a language of communication. The other language is the *Ethiopian Amharic* and the third is the *Arabic and the Berber Tanacheck* while the fourth is the *Liberian Vai*. These were not spoken within extensive wide areas and their circulation was limited.[13] Many other African languages had their own highly developed grammar and syntax but they were non-classical. The presence of the missionaries removed the illiteracy, which held back people from communicating with people from other places. People learnt to read and write some of the languages through the teachings that were held in schools founded by the missionaries. Invariably, literacy gained strong foothold in many parts of Africa through the pioneering work of the missionaries. Some of the Africans began to read the Bible in English and some in their own local languages translated by the foreign missionaries and their African partners.

One of the striking teachings of the Bible especially the New Testament is the worth and the dignity of the individual in the sight of God. All people are equal before God. This idea of equality of all humans before God influenced the policy of many developed nations that today champion the cause of Human Rights and the equality of all citizens before the Law. Many African converts influenced by this unique Christian view pioneered the crusade against colonial domination of Africans. According to African traditions, the individual person is counted in so far as he is a part of the group. The individual was dominated by fear of the group, the fear that comes from ignorance, superstition and belief in the existence of evil spirits.[14] The teachings of the Bible redeemed the Africans from the *personality-crushing* traditions and helped them to reassert their authentic selves above colonial domination and slavery. An African Christian understanding of the concept of *freedom and salvation* enshrined in the Bible, went beyond the moral and spiritual freedom often taught by many a political leader without applying it to practical daily administration of the law. The liberated African Christian rose above ethnic as well as colonial authority. While Christianity brought the African a new meaning and understanding of *freedom*, colonialism forced him to accept *servitude* and *domination* as his lot. In a subtle way, we can state that the *Mission of Christianity* in Africa influenced the nationalist struggle for independence in Africa. The early Christian missionaries did not set out to make Africans political and freedom fighters but invariably their teaching of freedom and God's love opened the eyes of many to the real essence of divine freedom and justice.

Although some missionaries displayed some overt acts of insult and abuse to the Africans, the basic massage they carried and taught was Freedom from sin, evil and oppression. This encouraged many young Africans who understood the Biblical teaching on the value of the individual freedom given to them by their Christian mission teachers.

Some African nationalists have misrepresented Christianity in many of their writings. Some called it an *oppressor, colonial agent, or intruder*, others saw it as an instrument of deception in the hands of foreign investors. People are free to hold whatever view they want about Christianity in Africa. It is generally believed that Christianity has helped more Africans improve their talents, achieve freedom and improve their living standard more than any other religious faith has done. Christianity laid an unconscious foundation for African Nationalism. Democracy, which many Africans shout for today, came as a result of Christian teaching and evangelisation. It is not preached or practised by any other religious systems in Africa. Christianity has done a lot of good by widening the scope of social relationships in the lives of those who accepted it in many parts of Africa. Many African Christians do not see themselves and their services in terms of the local community where they were born. European powers brought many unrelated tribal units together to form one country in many pats of Africa. As already said, they did this primarily for the administrative convenience of the European officers who colonized the territories. Those who were influenced by the teaching of Christianity in many of those countries are known to have been at the vanguard of the crusade for national unity in those countries. They did it without trying to make every citizen become a Christian. For instance, Christians in Ghana, Nigeria, Uganda, Kenya, Zambia, Tanzania and Namibia who have been struggling for national unity have never tried to force people from other faiths to become Christians. This is unlike what is happening in many countries where Muslims in those places would like their countries to be declared *Islamic Republics*. Many past Christian statesmen like Jomo Kenyatta of Kenya, Dr Nnamdi Azikiwe of Nigeria, Dr Sylvanus Olympio of Togo, Dr Nyerere of Tanzania and Dr Milton Obote of Uganda did not pressurise non-Christians in their countries to accept Christian faith or else lose their civic rights.

European exploitation brought in the Slave Trade, which depopulated Africa. Dr Bengt Sundkler stated that *it is estimated that the total number of slaves sold to European colonies amounted to between twenty and forty million*.[15] Kenneth Latourette's evaluation of the situation is even more shocking. According to him,

> *here was the most extensive exploitation of ones set of races by another which history has been...That this colossal evil was the work of people whose nominal faith was Christianity was an indictment of that religion which cannot be brushed aside*.[16]

Some African nationalist writers have unreservedly condemned the Christian Church as part of the clout that traded on human beings. But we still remember that contributions of Christian philanthropists and missionaries in the efforts to abolish trafficking on human beings. Sir F. Buxton's efforts in this respect are still current in our minds. It is a pity that few who nominally professed the faith were selfish enough to be involved in such sordid and inhuman trade which contradicted their faith. It is true that those selfish individuals did not represent the official stand and teaching of Christianity. Invariably, true Biblical Christianity did not support any form of slave trade. It is wrong to identify or associate every white man who sojourned in Africa as a Christian. This was the error that many Africans committed in the 18th and 19th centuries when missionaries were entering the hinterlands. Some Africans were shocked to see many unscrupulous European traders and soldiers get involved in sexual immorality with Black African women. Many of them had earlier known of men and women of integrity among the missionaries who lived among them in the villages.

The Aro Sub-group of the Igbo of Nigeria, for instance, exploited the presence of those unscrupulous white traders and wrecked their own indigenous people's economy and history. Shamelessly, the Aros built a civilisation that flourished between 1700 and 1850, a period that can be described as the *Dark Ages of Igbo History*. It was a civilization the Aros sustained on what could be described as **Machiavellian diplomacy, an open demonstration of how a black decadent civilization grew out of a white decadent civilization!** The Aros were not to blame for starting the Slave Trade. Western traders had to take the blame and many historians, economic and political philosophers have done that extensively. On the other hand, the Aros had to take the blame for their role in the trade that made their kith and kin commodities. The Slave Trade, above all, destroyed the first step the Igbo took to invent and develop the *Nsibidi* and *Aniocha* systems of writing. Both Scripts could have developed into international status if they had existed for a longer period and had served a wider generality of people instead of a closed Secret Society.

The essence of this short excursus is to state clearly that Christianity did not pioneer or encourage the Slave Trade, although few selfish individuals who nominally professed the faith got involved at one time or the other. The Christian patriot takes solace from the Bible that in spite of the weakness of human characters, even among the Church Leaders, Christianity itself offers a flawless rule and guide to life. Even the leaders would be subjected to the upright scrutiny of the Biblical injunction. If people were to take Christianity seriously, it stands for justice and peace, freedom and human rights. Invariably, the Bible upholds the Principles of Human Rights and there is no doubt that it condemns even the highly placed people for abuse Human Rights. The Prophet Nathan confronted King David directly on God's direction and instruction when the king committed adultery and planned the killing of Uriah in order to cover up his evil and dastardly sinful act. (2 Sam. 11 and 12.) Later we saw the prophet Elijah in frontal attack on King Ahab for dispossessing Naboth of his plot of land, even when he had promised to offer a substitute as an exchange. (1 Kings 21). The Christian Bible does not joke with the rights of the individual and is full of records of God's condemnation of even the most highly placed person for gross acts of injustice. This is unknown in many religious systems including Traditional African societies.

Christian nationalists who genuinely read and understood the Bible were encouraged to fight the rights of their oppressed people. The Bible-liberated African who saw that the Bible is the foundation on which Human Rights stood, began to enlarge his microcosm and reasserted himself, not only over tribal but also colonial authority. African Christians have stood against forces that denied them their freedom and self-esteem. For instance, the rise of many African Independent Churches had come up, among other reasons, as a result of the insults some intelligent African converts had in the Churches founded and administered by foreign missionaries. The leaders of those mission Churches did not allow indigenous Africans to take up responsible positions of leadership. This is true of the African Church, which broke away from the Anglican Church in Nigeria in the late 19th Century.

We must recognise some positive actions of the Christian Church in Africa. The Missionaries had generally stood against the oppressive colonial or traditional government in any place it existed. When the Government of the Union of South Africa introduced the new Native Laws Amendment Bill in 1957 which barred interracial gatherings of any kind, the late Archbishop Clayton, in collaboration with four other white bishops, wrote the Prime Minister, stressing the Church's condemnation of the bill. Part of the letter reads,

> The Church cannot recognise the right of an official of the secular government to determine whether or where a member of the Church of any race (who is not serving a sentence which restricts his freedom of movement) shall discharge his religious duty or participation in public worship...Bishops, priests and laymen are represented without distinction of race or colour.[17]

Many other Christians in high positions of trust took similar stand against Slave Trade and Apartheid Government. The Roman Catholic and other Christian denominations made open condemnation of racial discrimination and Apartheid in those days in South Africa. Bishop Vernon Inman of Natal, was often heard to say,

> As a Church, we loathe and abominate the devilish device known as apartheid and we believe it is leading our country to ultimate ruin...We continue to oppose it as unchristian.[18]

Christian Churches took this stand against social ills and have not changed their position any where and at any time. There were, however, occasions when some individual Christians behaved badly and acted against the official stand of the Church. Western education introduced by the church generated some awareness in many African Christians who turned back to use their opportunities to fight for the freedom of their people. They thus, became the forerunners and pioneers of African Nationalism. Many of such nationalists came from Church circles. The studied history, civics, philosophy and theology. The study of history, for instance, placed very powerful weapons in the hands of many literate Africans. We know that historical consciousness was one of the chief elements that motivated African nationalism. The literate Africans studied courses, gained ideas and imbibed some philosophical principles that later helped them to fight against foreign domination. The Christian missionaries introduced educational and religious literature, liberal arts and humanities. Those among other things provided wide opportunities to many Africans and broadened their minds. Many of those young people could have died illiterate local leaders but the opportunity of Western education and enlightenment offered by the Church enhanced their chances. Although the Church did not intentionally set out to train nationalists and political activists for Africa, the foundation of education they laid opened wider opportunities for young Africans and generated the spirit of nationalism in a good number of them. Indirectly, the Church could be said to have laid the foundation for the spirit of nationalism in Africa.

7.6   Conclusion

We have presented Christianity here as if it were a flawless and perfect institution. Obviously it is but the fault of human weaknesses had abused the good intensions and programmes of the Christian faith itself. It is the imperfect human whose own nature has tried to weaken the strength of Christianity. Some individuals have not demonstrated the total Christian qualities in their dealings with their fellows. Their weakness is personal and not that of the Faith they tend to represent. The weakness is not in Christianity but in the people. Christianity is so complete in itself that in spite of human weaknesses, history has it that many progressive programmes in human society still owe their foundation and development to Christian origin.

From what recorded history has accredited to Christian presence in the development of many parts of the world, Africa stands to benefit from such experience if people would allow Christian principles to influence and direct their lives. Many countries can develop the mental and environmental background on which lasting democracy would thrive if eternal virtues of Christianity are used to shape the African society. Unfortunately, many countries are still operating on the traditional moral and philosophical foundations but outwardly look like they are operating on strong foundation of principles of Christian morality. Although many countries in the West which embraced Christianity several centuries ago had failed at one point in time or the other in their efforts to build stable and clean society, there are still elements of development and sense of direction in their body politic. Christianity may not be openly professed but most of the ethical norms had been deeply rooted in Christian tradition. The initial foundations of nationhood of those countries which were laid on strong Christian principles are today leading them to a type of life that is directed with moral values, that seek public interest and development of the society as a top priority.

Africa was one of the leading centres of development in the Ancient World. She was one of the Cradles of Civilization but unfortunately that form of civilisation did not stand the test of time. She lost that civilisation and now needs to build on a new foundation which will bring her to the level of modern world system. Many other glorious empires of the ancient world collapsed. Greek and Roman Empires collapsed. Yet both Greece and Italy are not counted today as poor and underdeveloped world. They lost their past glorious empires and yet picked up the relics and are today marching on with the rest of the developed world. It is clear that many of the modern developed countries of the world are not standing on the foundation of their traditional ancestral cultures. Those countries which embraced the *transforming power* of Christianity overtook the civilisations that stuck to their *primary world view*. No ideological principles, philosophical and economic theory could be compared with the *transforming power* of Christianity in human society.

On a very dogmatic note, any people who persistently reject the eternal virtues of Christian faith and teaching would continue to lag behind other nations of the world. We do not say this to offend any one or to compel people to become Christians, but to state the fact that there is need to allow elements that shaped other societies to cast the same light of development on some one who is seriously looking for growth and development in line with others. This does not mean that Africa should copy European or American brand of development but to allow some objective Christian moral principles to influence her basic way of doing things. The present form of Christianity manifesting itself in Africa today is still scratching on the surface. The African heart is still deeply rooted in Traditional African Religion and most of the manifestations of noisy Christianity today are *mere cosmetics* that do not change people's life style. Corruption is still at the base of the heart of the people and society.

Africa can work out her own form of Christianity by allowing some valuable and noble elements in her culture go through the transforming influence of Christianity and use them to reshape her focus and though-pattern. African experience and methodology may be peculiar to her needs and resources. Yet such should not wrench the heart of the Christian Gospel. The **accidence** may be different but the **essence** would be the same unchanging word of God. It is still a fact of history that many international Human Rights Organizations find less abuse of human rights in countries with strong Christian background than in other societies. For instance, it is easy to criticise a democratic government of some countries and get away with it. An individual has a right to criticise some aspects of the policy or laws of his country without paying dearly for it. Yet this type of Freedom is not enjoyed in many nations of the world today. There is no country today that can be termed Christian Republic or Christian Country but those countries that have had long tradition of Christian influence seem to allow a form of freedom that gives every citizen the rights to what the United Nations describes as Fundamental Human Rights. It is not so in all the countries of the world today. Christianity has in effect opened peoples' eyes and minds to the great developmental process of the world.

NOTES

1.	see Acts 2: 7 – 10.	*Revised Standard Version of the Bible.*
2.	Aylward Shorter.	*African Christian Theology.* Gt Britain, Geoffrey Chapman, 1975, p, 6

3. J. S. Mbiti (ed)   Confessing Christ in Different Cultures. (Switzerland, WCC Publications 1977, pp. 177 - 179

4. J.F. A. Ajayi   *Christian Missions in Nigeria, 1841 – 1891: The making of a new elite.* London, Longmans Publications, 1965.

5. T. F. Buxton   *The African Slave Trade and its remedy.* London, 1840. pp 282, 511.

6. J.F. A Ajayi   ibid. p. 11

7. U. R. Onunwa   Christian Missionary methods and their influence in Eastern Nigeria, in E. E. Metuh, (ed.) Gods *in Retreat: Continuity and Change in African Religions.* Enugu Nigeria: Fourth Dimension Publishers, 1986, p. 78

8. E. J. Berg.   The Character and Prospects of African Economics in W. Goldschidt (ed) *The United States and Africa.* London and New York, Fredrick Praeger, Inc 1963, pp. 117

9. E.J. Berg   ibid. p. 116

10. R. Walker   *The Holy Ghost Fathers.* Dublin: Rock College, 1933, p. 80

11. _____   ibid. p. 116

12. H. Butterfield   *Christianity in European History.* London, 1952. pp 19 – 21

13. N. Sithole.   African Nationalism. 2nd Edition. London, O.U.P. 1959. P. 84

14. _____   ibid. p. 85 – 86

15. Bengt Sundkler.   The World Mission. Trans. Eric J. Sharpe. Grand Rapids, Win.B Eerdmans Publishing Co. 1966, p. 147.

16. K.S. Latourette   A History of the Expansion of Christianity. Grand Rapids, Zondervan Publishing House, 1970, p. 320

17. Cited by N. Sithole   op.cit. p. 88

18. _____   op.cit. p. 88

CHAPTER EIGHT
Analysis and Conclusion

We began by stating that Africa which used to host one of the *Cradles of Civilization* in the Ancient World was described by early European visitors as a *Dark Continent*. They based their description on the state of things they saw in the continent when they arrived. Africa did not measure to the standard of *development* they had back home in their countries. Yet Africa experienced several forms of highly developed art and culture in the prehistoric time ere the arrival of Europeans. The *Nationalist writers* claim that it was the conquest of Africa by the Europeans that left her *underdeveloped*. She lost her long established cultural artefacts, and wealth to those who invaded her. Her present state of *underdevelopment* is a factor of European *expansionism and colonization*. Africa has moved from the state of *Dark Continent* to that of *Developing Nations or Third World*. All these new names are polite ways of stating that Africa is still backward, underdeveloped and *primitive* when compared with the *developed and industrialized nations* of the world. She is one of the poorest continents in the world with the lowest Gross National Income per capita. From all the definitions of *development and underdeveloped* which we have already looked at, Africa does not fit adequately into the internationally accepted standard of *developed peoples of the world. She is yet to develop.*

African writers and Black Nationalists point accusing fingers on the Europeans as the *chief architects and agents of African Underdevelopment.* We have already outlined some of the great monumental establishments in Africa ere her contact with European visitors, merchants, explorers, missionaries and colonial administrators. Taking up how Africa developed before the coming of the Europeans who *underdeveloped* Africa, Rodney articulated distinguishing areas of culture where Africa had reached a pinnacle of achievement before her contact with Europeans.[1] Probably, he was referring to *oral tradition, literature, myths , arts and sculpture* but certainly not in heavy industrialization, scientific discovery, and abstract mathematical way of thinking. The nationalists see European presence in Africa from the point of view of exploitation, and underdevelopment of the continent for the good of the Europeans themselves. Their presence brought nothing good for the people. On the other hand, many Europeans saw their presence as *a civilizing mission*. This is particularly true of the   Christian Missionaries whose services to the people were purely humanitarian. Although nobody will ever under-rate or gloss over the ills of European conquest of Africa, one must not also forget some other valuable things that came out of the whole enterprise. There is need to be cautious so as to know where to draw the line. The conquest of Africa was not the only reason for the present state of things in the continent. It goes far beyond that. The present work goes far into the history of the *development of African thought pattern, world view, traditions and religious culture which determine and guide the way of the growth of a people and their civilization*. We must come to a point of looking for the cause of our problems beyond the immediate agents. Although the immediate cause may be an important agent, the underlying and basic foundation must be seen as far more important. That is why we have in this work stated that it is the traditional religion and culture of Africa more than any other agent that has caused the present state of *underdevelopment*. This does not, in any way justify the wicked acts of Slave Trade and the evils of colonization.

There are two ways of looking at things. The first is to see the presence of Western countries in Africa purely from the nationalist dogmatic perspective. This means that the Europeans came to Africa to the detriment of the African, and any benefits from the contact might have been purely accidental. The Europeans did not come to *develop Africa* but to *exploit and underdevelop her* in the interest of the Europeans. Africans did not invite them for assistance. They were victims of a more conquering power. According to Ali Mazrui, European ambitions were of course varied. They changed with times and circumstances. There was interest in new sources of raw materials, new potential markets for European manufactured goods, once a demand was cultivated and purchasing power created, new outlet for European surplus population regardless of the new crisis of habitability in parts of Africa, new potential source of energy with all those waterfalls and subsequently with all the coal, uranium... new souls to convert to Christianity, in short the new world to conquer.[2] We could see this as a comprehensive analysis of the motivations for the European adventure. But was it the original aim of the first explorers and adventurers? Why did Africans themselves not embark on similar adventure to other parts of the world? Did their *microcosmic world view* allow them to visualize such a world? Taking Ali

Mazrui's stance a little further, some nationalists singled out Christianity and criticized it adversely. They saw it as a *mechanism devised by Europeans to steal away the valuable treasures from Africa*. Thus while *Africans were praying as the Missionaries taught them to, the European merchants and administrators were preying on them*. Besides, Western education, the handmaid of Christianity had two killing effects on Africa. When the Europeans saw that it was effective in subduing the minds of Africans, the colonial government joined in introducing it into Africa. Initially the Christian Missions alone established school before the colonial government joined. The two dangerous effects of Western Education introduced by Christianity stood out clearly. First, it corrupted the thinking and sensibilities of the African and filled him with complexes. Thus it made the African become negative and hostile to African traditional religion and culture. The African began to hate things *African*. This is the *denurturing effect of Western Education* on Africans. The second is that it left the African a *split personality- neither the West nor his authentic self*. These views need to be balanced.

We know the altruistic and vicarious sufferings of many missionaries who threw away their lives in Africa serving the people. Dr Kwame Nkrumah, a frontline nationalist and the first executive President of Ghana who fought against European and particularly Christian orientation of Africans made a very objective and insightful remarks on the role of the missionaries in one of his papers. He paid glowing tribute to the missionaries when he addressed the delegates of International Missionary Conference meeting at Accra Ghana in 1957. According to him:

> *If you have time to visit more widely in this country you will often find as you travel along the roads, little cemeteries lost in the bush where lie buried the brave men and women who in bringing the Christian faith to this country, gave the last full measure of their devotion. They knew they faced the certainty of loneliness and imminent risk of death. Yellow fever decimated them and their families. But they still came. They belong to the martyrs of Christianity as surely as those who faced persecution for their faith. The fortitude which they showed is the sure foundation upon which your work has been based. Ghana salutes these men and women who gave their lives for the enlightenment and welfare of their land.*[3]

In the above tribute, Dr Nkrumah did not mince words in acknowledging the services and sacrifices of Christian missionaries to Africa .We must try to distinguish between a fraudulent merchant and explorer who came for his own good and a genuine volunteer who came for the love of God embraced in Christianity. It is difficult for one who has not experienced the love of Christ to understand what sacrifice for the good of others means. The present writer is not out to do an apologetic defence on behalf of Christian Missionaries, some of whom died several years ago. The important thing is to put every detail in its historical context.

The other effect of the European presence is to see it an outright and auspicious blessings which brought Africa to the main stream of modern world affairs. The *Euro-centric view* is to uphold and praise every European activity and programme in Africa as flawless and perfect, an impeccable civilizing project aimed at the good of the Africans. This view is somewhat distorted and ignores other facts of history in the whole package. This is the view of some European writers and their African *wards* who wanted to please the audience for which they wrote. A few objective writers among the Europeans came up to dismiss this view in order to balance facts. Harris Mobley had objectively classified the writings from indigenous African scholars [particularly those from Ghana] into two broad categories. The first is what he called the *Literature of Tutelage* in which African scholars presented the views that would please and impress their European mentors and benefactors. The other is the *Critique* written by those Africans considered representatives of responsible leadership in both community and state who demonstrated concern for both the faults and the merits of the missionaries.[4] It is within the two extreme positions that a balanced assessment falls— bringing out the strength and weakness of European presence in Africa in an objective way.

Walter Rodney had lucidly explained that African culture was at the peak of its development before the European presence shattered it and *stole* some of its valuable parts. It is the present writer's view that the traditional religion and culture which nourished the society, *controlled, directed and predicted* the way things go in Africa was not as *development - conscious* as some nationalists have made it. It is therefore the traditional religion and culture more than any other factor that is responsible for the problem of *underdevelopment of Africa*. It has the potentials to start a project but cannot go far enough because of its microcosmic perception of the world. It cannot project far and therefore cannot stand the onslaught of a more conquering culture. All hope is not lost. Africa can still get up and join the race for *development* through the absorptions and integration of Christianity which transformed the Western world into what it is today.

We have developed this thesis from an inter-disciplinary perspective-with data gleaned from history, education, economics, political science, anthropology, linguistics, sociology, religion and philosophy. Oral materials obtained from many living votaries of the traditional religion and culture were supplemented with documented evidence from archives, journals, books and museums in Africa and Europe. Some living votaries of the traditional religion and culture especially in Tanzania and Kenya hailed Christian missionaries to their place as purveyors of development, progress and civilization. A clear descriptive presentation of the principal elements of the traditional religion shows that Africa has an authentic religious faith but it is important to allow Christianity to pass through it and refine, purify and utilize valuable elements in building a progressive and egalitarian society. The sordid rituals inherent in the traditional culture must be expunged if Africa will join the *League of developed nations* which allowed the transforming power of Christianity to refine their indigenous culture.

Nature supplied all the basic needs of the traditional Africans. They lived so close to nature that they did not bother themselves about things that were not within their reach. All that they needed were within easy reach. Their contact with a *conquering culture* shattered their world and exposed them to multi-dimensional phenomenon. They had to grapple with problems of *extension of scale* The newly enlarged cosmos exposed them to a lot of other attendant problems even though many other values came from such new experiences. It is within these new experiences that Western education falls. No matter the criticisms people may have against it, Africans came into a new world where they could easily communicate with people from other parts of the world and even from other parts of their own continent and countries.

By presenting the Traditional Religion and Culture as a factor of *Underdevelopment of Africa*, we have *ispo facto*, inferred that Christianity is a harbinger of development. It enhanced human values and built ones that brought humanity out of the *darkness of the primitive age*. We have used history of transformation of Western Europe to illustrate that Christianity is a catalyst that accelerated the rate of human development in the world. Although we have presented the Traditional Religion and Culture of Africa as the chief agent of *underdevelopment*, we shall not fail to heed the call by a new group of African scholars in recent times. The group appreciates the weaknesses of the traditional religion and culture but at the same time underlines some valuable aspects that we need to preserve. In a well outlined article, the group drew our attention to the valuable contributions some non-material cultural elements in our contemporary world can make towards the anticipated development of Africa. The functions of *non-material culture* touch on the very life of the people and cannot be done away with. If anyone tries to do away with such very important aspect of culture, the one will endanger the lives of the practitioners and owners of the traditional culture. There is no way to do away with such elements with out the lives of the Africans being in danger of total extinction. For instance, such elements guide behaviours, and exert social control in society, mould social personality, distinguish one society from the other, interpret and integrate the values and institutions of the society and charge them with meaning. Such elements furnish the basis for social solidarity, reserve legitimate cultural accretion and development from time to time.[5] The modern scholar has a big task. He must work diligently to decipher what those elements are in every society he intends to study. It is not easy for a casual researcher to understand the nature and characteristics of those *non-material elements* which the scholars have drawn our attention to. For instance, it may be the myth of origin, proverbs, or any other form of oral saga that circulate in the various subculture areas. It is only a close study of each society that can reveal such non-classical valuable elements that each society guards with jealous care.

We must emphasize from the experiences of the field work that many of the scholars who praise the small scale societies have rarely lived in them. Anyone who has deeply been involved in field work in rural communities in Africa would come out with different ideas from the imaginary pictures which the arm-chair scholars paint. Those who try to romanticise the African past should put it in its historical context. We shall not use the abuse of Christian civilization by corrupt European social climbers and opportunists to assess the ideals of Christianity. It is the responsibility of the honest and committed Christian teacher to educate the people and to show them the way forward. But certainly, many patriotic Africans who long for the *old good days* act like the mythical *Peter Pan* who lived for many years but refused to grow. They reject the responsibility and enlargement of scales and often forget what the tiny societies of the past looked like. They need to be reminded that the *Noble Savage in Acardia* is a dream and not reality. Some of the problems we complain of in today's world are parts of the results of the abuse of *development* which can be avoided if handled with caution.

They are not beyond human control. Many of us who have lived as field research workers in remote African villages still have our experiences of the type of morality and hospitality we often encountered. William Bosman whom we had earlier discussed remarked that:

> *The Negroes are... crafty... and very seldom to be trusted, being sure to slip no opportunities of cheating any European or indeed one another...* [6]

He did not exaggerate matters in this remark. Some of the children and adults who see us in the field think that we are *rich men sent by the Government* with excess money which can be spent anyhow. We are therefore people from whom they could extort money and many other gifts, after all the money we are to spend does not belong to us but to the *impersonal Government* With this notion, prices of goods are hiked in the local shops and markets especially when they discover that we cannot speak the local language. Often some of our local guides and interpreters do not return our change when we send them to buy us things from the markets. The local taxi drivers take longer routes in order to make us pay higher fares. Those who hail the traditional African villages and communities as beacons of morality do not balance their views properly. After examining the features of the traditional religion and culture, and participating in some of its rituals, I can conclude without fear of contradict-ion that some elements of Traditional religions and culture pose a hindrance to serious intellectual activity especially in the area of scientific creativity and innovation. This is not to damage the personality and dignity of the African but to create an awareness in him to look for solution to the perennial problem of *underdevelopment*.

Traditional African science existed quite alright in some form or the other but the social customs of most African cultures and religion were such that knowledge was largely treated as a valuable commodity which should be hoarded and therefore guarded jealously in much the same way as material possession.[7] Certainly, knowledge could not grow and circulate freely in small scale traditional society with its microcosmic features. Christianity with its vibrant zeal for mission distributes ands hawks itself in such a way that good news, progress and love are multiplied when they are shared. A non-missionary religion like African Traditional Religion and Culture has nothing to show the outside world to copy. It hoards its knowledge and its scientific discoveries and inventions and in the process cannot be exported to the outside world to share. This is one of the major causes of *underdevelopment and stagnation of knowledge*. The educational influence of Christianity developed the level of literacy in Africa. The local languages were committed to writing and many people today can boast of having their cultural heritage and values preserved in documented forms. If African societies would grow and develop, they should not only be attached to a dynamic and vibrant faith like Christianity, but must as a matter of fact, allow Christianity to do to them what it did to the *traditional pagan cultures of Europe which it transformed*.

NOTES

1. W. Rodney, *How Europe underdeveloped Africa.*[London: Bogle-Le Ouverture Publications 1972], p.4

2. Kwame Nkrumah — An address to the International Assembly of Missionary Council meeting in Accra Ghana, 1957. Quoted by John Pobee *The Church in Africa, 1977*

3. Ali Mazrui — *The African Condition: The Reith Lectures* .[London, Heineman, 1982], p 32

4. H.W. Mobley — *The Ghanaian Image of the Missionary.* [Leiden: E.J. Brill Publishers 1970] pp. 2 & 7

5. N.S.S Iweh — *Christianity, Culture and Colonization.* [PortHarcourt –Nigeria College of Education Press, 1985], p 58

6. U.R. Onunwa — *The Study of African Traditional Religion in Time – Perspective* [Unpub. Ph.D.thesis,University of Nigeria, Nsukka,1984],p 58

7. S.E. Okoye — Traditional African Language as a medium of scientific Creativity and Innovation , in O.U. Kalu, [ed]*African Cultural Development.*[Enugu-Nigeria: Fourth Dimension Publishers, 1978], p. 256

THE EPILOGUE
The Challenge of African Nationalism

Dr Aggrey, one of the outstanding West African scholars of his time and a front-line nationalist one said that *I am proud of my colour and he who is not proud of his colour is not worthy to live*. When he left his native land, Gold Coast, [the present Ghana] to study in the United States of America, it was the time racial discrimination, based on human skin, was at its peak.

For such a dark-skinned young man to own up and stand firm on what he knew to be right, was a mark of self confidence that led to the growth of national awareness and growth. Such moves laid the foundation for the national independence of the colonies from their foreign rulers Except Liberia that was a different establishment and rehabilitation of repatriated slaves, Ghana was the first West African country to gain political independence from Colonial rule. Other nationalists in that category included E.Wilmot Blyden, J.E. Casely Hayford, Samuel Lewis, J.B. Horton, John M Sarba, J. Abanyomi Cole, P.J. Meffre, Mojola Agbebi. They were true to *their colour* not only in their fight against European exploitation of Africa but also in their refusal to enrich themselves through dishonest means. We should not see the idea of nationalism only in the sense of fighting against outside invaders of Africa but could also include regular internal review and self-examination of ways of life that can retard growth of stable and lasting democracy and development. A true nationalist should speak out against any element that can constitute impediments to *individual and national development*. This second perspective is what we have adopted in this study. Many Human Rights Organizations in Africa fighting against abuse of Human Rights in the countries are true *nationalists* if they have no other ulterior motives. We often say that *truth is bitter*, but one must say it if it is going to lead to progress and correction of ills. Many sycophants would not like offending any people because they do not want to antagonize anyone. One of the greatest problems a human being can face is that of *a self-criticism*. Anyone who comes to that stage in life is really getting to a level of maturity and is true to himself. He has come to a stage where he will stop blaming others for his setback or misfortune. He sits back, reviews his strategy and approach, adjusts a few things, and begins again. He does not succumb to the threats and fear of failure. To him, *failure* is just *success delayed*.

The African nationalist of our time, are they academic theorists, political activists, religious experts, economic analysts and the common masses, should come up in sincerity to seek answers to the endemic complex problem of *Underdevelopment*. When it seems a stable democracy is taking roots in one country, a new military dictatorship will strike in the next door neighbour the following day. There is continuous change of government that often leads to fruitless and senseless civil wars. A *monocausal explanation* may look too narrow and limited to give enough room for a broad-based long term answers and solution. We will instead suggest a *multi causal and multidimensional explanation*. What we have done here may look like *a monocausal explanation* through religio-cultural approach. In the true sense of the African Worlds, *religion is the underpinner of the cosmology*. Every aspect of African life hinges on African Traditional Religion and Culture. It permeates all aspects of life, economics. politics, education, agriculture, psychology, social relationships, etc. So in effect, by taking *Religio-Cultural Perspective*, we are indirectly taking a *multidimensional approach*. This does not, however stop experts in other fields of life to come up with contributions from their own micro-disciplines. Socio-historical factors are as important as religio-missiological factors.

The greatness in a human life does not lie in not falling but in being able to rise again after a fall. They had dislocated African past and it had experienced many falls. So it had been with many *developed nations* of our present world. Their history if full of *rise and fall*, yet they did not give up, but at each time making use of every good opportunity. That opportunity has equally come to Africans through Christianity. Many past kingdoms and empires had crumbled. Many other obscure societies had, on the other hand, risen to prominence. It is a paradox of *light and darkness, sadness and joy, rise and fall. The challenge* of the new spirit of *Nationalism* should be the total *emancipation and development* of Africa from poverty, illiteracy, political instability, economic stagnation and dependency. Often those who parade themselves as nationalists have other motives - acquisition of power and wealth. They come under the guise of *national redemption* but end worse than the so called *corrupt government* they overthrew. Invariably and unfortunately, some learned academics and politicians have used their positions to enrich themselves - and by so doing bringing their people and country to a stage of *underdevelopment*. They feed fat and live in grotesque wealth while millions of their people starve. Some self-styled champions of *African Nationalism* have ended up *looting their countries' wealth* and hiding them in foreign banks with the help of some unscrupulous foreign partners. More often than not, a military coup d'etat which sets out on a cleansing mission ends up with rich and corrupt *Generals whose personal bank accounts overseas* are bigger than that of the country.

Although the present writer has suggested Christianity as the Religion that can offer *the much needed development* in Africa, he is not talking of a type that will want to turn Africans into spurious Americans or Europeans but instead the Biblical Christianity that

Will grow as African Churches and not as extensions of parishes and bishoprics...They must be allowed to take roots in the soil of the African culture in which they are planted...[1]

This is important because we have already stated that Christianity is different from Western Culture or American Culture. Yet it expressed itself through those cultures. African Christianity will bear the stamp of originality and yet maintain its Catholicity. It must be a Church that is *people-centred and people - oriented*. At the regional or national levels, rural development, industrialization and urbanization must be made a top priority. Church members and their leaders should contribute spiritual insights and also material resources for the good of the people. Primal and Christian ideas about man, nature and community will frequently prove to be allies for facing new challenges. Such challenges may put Christians in positions of taking difficult decisions and contributing hard physical labour in finding ways to share the main sources of wealth such as land, water, forests and minerals. Christians may also be involved in common decision making bodies that are responsible for programmes that will benefit from an enlarged national labour force through careful labour planning. The interest of the individual may be substantially determined by that of the nation as a whole, since the basic aspirations of the community are those of its members and the concern of each individual those of the community as a whole.[2] A Church so committed to the cause of African *development* will not be a *fanatical exclusive sect* but a Church, though in fellowship with the World wide Communion of Christian family, will bear a mark of African identity in polity, theology and liturgy. It will not be a neo-colonialist agent that gives African

Christians a false sense of humility and piety and makes them perpetual babes in the faith and will forever depend on foreign missions for aid, development of its polity, liturgy and theology. It is a Church that is authentically Biblical, indigenous and Christ- centred. It should not be turned into a hypocritical *money-making industry* which some preachers seem to make it look like today.

There is a growing number of enlightened and educated Africans who are manifesting their *nationalism* in a subtle but rather obscure and *backwards -looking* way. Many of them have adopted some secular beliefs and ideologies in their bid to project Africa as a growing and progressive continent. A good number of them is showing keen interest in the traditional African art and culture without necessarily opting for full membership in African Traditional Religion and Culture. Some of them show appreciation and enthusiasm for the revival of cultural festivals and rituals They were responsible for the Second World Black and African Festival of Arts and Culture [FESTAC] hosted by Nigeria in 1977.

It scored a point by bringing to life the ancient cultural artefacts and events of the Black race in Africa and in Diaspora. We are yet to reap the fruits of that *international jamboree in Africa* in terms of its implications for *development* and improvement of standard of living for the Africans.

The ideological preoccupation of many Africans have led us now to ask again the question that many people have been asking since the dawn of national independence in many countries. The question is *Whither Africa, or Which way Africa?* The answer is important now more than ever before if we do not want Africa of the 21st Century to suffer again like she did in the past. This is a problem that concerns every African and the Black race world wide because the continent hosts about 25% of the world's population. An ideological frame of thought must be worked out and Africa must do it for herself. Her large number of children must liberate her from the *doldrums of economic, political, social, technological and religious backwardness.* Any ideological principle that sets Africa against God will evidently fail. Africans are incurably religious and Christianity should fill that *religious space for future.*

Many people had in the past suggested some ways to come out of this backwardness. Some strategies were tried. They include joining the West or the East when the East was a strong Power Block. Others opted for *Principles of Non-Alignment* with a common attitude of *no permanent friend and no permanent foe, but permanent interest.* Should Africa go West and borrow her capitalism or to East and imbibe her *dead Communism?* Capitalism had been on the scene for a much longer time than Communism. Both systems have been used to a considerable extent to solve human problems. In other words, both systems have been used to help human beings in their various sections of the world where they are practised. Before the *death of Communism* in Soviet Union a few years ago, it was effective in the Eastern Block though not to be equally matched with Capitalism practised in the West, for instance in the Great Britain and the United States of America, which are inherently Christian in orientation.

If we take *functionalism or pragmatism* as our objective index of evaluation, both systems worked in the *development of the areas where they existed and is more developed than Africa.* Out of *deep nationalism*, Africans are divided in their lines of approach- pro capitalist West or pro-communist. Since Communism has failed in many African countries in recent past, it does not seem to have great advocates currently.

Capitalism, by its implication means that all factors of production will remain in the hands of private individuals. In highly industrialized societies, there might be no difficulty in operating this but in Africa, there is no such *property* or *capital* of which to speak. The real capital will continue to be in the hands of foreign investors in spite of the fact of *nationalization and privatization* going on in many African countries. Do they really affect the rural communities and the poor masses in society? If foreign investors and a few rich citizens own the capital in partnership, it will in turn mean that most of the economy of the continent will continue to be controlled by foreign experts who will invariably control the political systems. In actual sense of life, *Who rules Africa- her own indigenous sons and daughters or remote foreign powers who pay the piper and call the tune?* This is the sad situation that has been revolving for so many years in Africa since the post colonial era. Other implications of whatever choice that is made exist and are well known but suffice it to say that free enterprise in any African country is bound to expose the *capital-lacking* Africans to the mercy of foreigners who have the capital and by that continue the trends of exploitation.

On the other hand, Communism has now collapsed in the East and has left the people in many difficulties. When it was in force in many parts of the Soviet Union, it created *regimentation* that many *micro-ethnic* groups in Africa had never been subjected to before they were forcefully merged by the colonial powers with other groups into *nation-states.*

Many Africans who had never been subjected to any such external rules to achieve order and peace in society may resist the regimental measures that

Communism adopts to enforce its principles. Some people may see it as a new form of slavery. Those who had just come out of the tyrannical powers of military government may resist it. Freedom-loving Africans may oppose the tyrannical rule of Communism. The African pattern of land tenure is too *sacred* to be removed from its religious undertone which Communism may introduce and any likely compulsory acquisition of land for *industrial development* under any Socialist regime would be resisted by many people. The problem of *atheism*, also is a serious one. The Godless philosophy of Communism is abhorrent to African way of thinking. Anyone who will project that type of ideology in Africa can only succeed for a short time with a strong army to impose it on the people who will eventually resist it.

Africa has not fully accepted any of the systems as a *panacea* to her many problems. She may in her own interest evolve a third alternative system that may suit her own experiences, special needs and temperament. She is, however *flirting* with the ideas that look auspicious at a time and later swing on to any other convenient one. For sure, the instability of government is one reason for the situation. Meanwhile, the *non-alignment* policy is not a permanent *escape route* devised by African nations to play on chance but an interim measure taken while waiting to evolve her own policy that may depend primarily on a number of other factors. She is meanwhile satisfied with borrowing from both the West and the decadent East. Some African countries are trying to develop a form of *Socialism* indigenous to them but this is yet to get strong roots. The experiment in Zimbabwe is still in its elementary stage.

No ideological principle or policy alien to the African peoples in its totality would last nor could any system imposed from outside make any lasting impact. That is the problem with the type of *Democracy that the West* wants to establish in many African countries. African ideas of *Democracy* are totally different. The African nationalists who want Africa to *develop into a modern self-sufficient continent* should always bear in mind that no principles with *foreign accretion* can take roots in Africa. Any attempt by leaders to rush their countries to accept a particular form of ideology may end in crises. This is where the task of choice comes in. We have suggested that Christianity properly related to African-felt needs will be worthwhile principle. None of the Eastern or Western views in its unmodified state can serve any useful purpose in the present quest for means to develop Africa.

What aspects of the Traditional Religion and Culture shall we adopt in our quest to build a new Africa? We can suggest some that we consider valuable after a long period of field work in different parts of the continent. Each section may have its own peculiar features but there are some aspects that run across all the communities. Nevertheless, what right have we to choose for the votaries of the religion and culture the very aspects to retain or remove. That is the error of many early functionalist anthropologists who adopted purely *functionalist stance* in their study of African Cultures and Religion. Many nationalists who are anxiously proposing the revival of African cultures have not sat down to select the one to revive and those to throw away as unnecessary and unhelpful. The exercise needs a dispassionate action because wrong choices may affect many people not yet born.

We will like to explore more on the skill of the traditional Africa especially they had the skill that they used in the development of iron and copper several centuries before contact with the Europeans and Arabs was made. The Nok Culture of Northern Nigeria had been in existence before any known contacts were made. Some cottage industries that produced farming and household equipments need to be recaptured before the elders die out. Those locally based could form the nucleus of any meaningful industrial project that can take off in any part of Africa. Major industrial projects could take off from there. Africans in contemporary period should not hope or wait for any *transfer of technology* from the European to them since the later knows the overwhelming long term implications. Iron and steel industries in Africa would take off only when Africans begin to explore the methods themselves. That will be the origin of development of *Technological Villages in different parts of Africa.*

Christianity in Africa should therefore come up to grip with the traditional notion of *wholeness*. There is no clear distinction between indigenous African's religious ideas, beliefs, practice, and other aspects of his life. John S. Mbiti has aptly described the African as *notoriously* religious. This is the aspect of African life that Christianity should take up seriously. For instance, many people who claim to be Christians in Africa today, contradict themselves with disgusting ethical behaviour.

Besides, noble African symbols should not only be accepted but also used in *nation building*. Pope Pius XII in his *Papal Encyclical letter*, on promoting Catholic Mission overseas, warned several years ago that:

> *The Church from the beginning down to our own time has always followed*
> *this wise practice: Let not the Gospel on being introduced into any new land*

destroy or extinguish whatever its people possess that is naturally good, just or beautiful... Whatever is not inseparably bound up with superstition and error will always receive kindly consideration and when possible will be preserved in the text...[3]

The modern Church in Africa should follow this agelong advice from a man of God who tried in his own time to see that the light of the Gospel reached every part of the world. It means that those who want to *develop Africa* can still explore some valuable African symbols, cultural artefact, non-material cultural elements and systems that will enhance their work. In our new quest for materials and methods for the *development* of Africa, we cannot *drop the tools from the air*. They will come from the existing cultural milieu. African development *must take roots* from the African soil. We cannot *transfer technology* or *transport it from abroad*. It must be groomed and nurtured here. Our African indigenous thought must be focussed and directed along this line.

There is, therefore, an urgent need to seek the *roots* of African Culture and unearth what is good and beautiful in it and effectively   convert it to the *African model of development* we want. This does not need to be patterned on European, Asian or North American model. This does not preclude the use of materials from such sources. This is the task educated African should initiate and all hands must be on deck. This is the sort of transformation Christianity did in many countries and can do so in Africa.

NOTES

1.   J.H. Nketia   The contributions of African Culture to Christian Worship. *International Review of Mission* XLVII, [1958], p. 268

2.   This does not mean reverting to a crude traditional system where the individual right has no pride of place nor a situation where *self* is projected above the common good. A situation where the life of an individual is respected and the entire community also preserved is necessary.

3.   Pope Pius XII,   *Encyclical Letter, 1961.*

BIBLIOGRAPHY

A - Theories of Development and Underdevelopment

Amaucheazi, E. C.	*Readings in Social Science.* Enugu, Fourth Dimension Publishers, 1980
Aschcraft, N.	*Colonisation and Underdevelopment.* NY, 1973
Bartlett, F.	Religion as Experience and Action in *Riddel Memorial Lectures* London, Oxford University Press, 1950
Berberough, B.	The Meaning of Underdevelopment: A critique of Mainstream Theories of Development and Underdevelopment. *Quarterly Journal of School of International Studies.* Vol. 17, No. 1 (Jan – March, 1978.)
Bradbury, R.E.	*The Benin Kingdom of the Edo-Speaking Peoples of South-*

Western Nigeria

Cole, J.P.	*The Development Gap: A spatial analysis of world poverty and inequality.* Leicester, 1981
Curtin, P.D.	*The Image of Africa: British Ideas and Action 1780 – 1850.* Wisconsin, Wisconsin University Press, 1964
Curle, A.	*Education for Liberation.* London, Tavistock, 1973
Elkan, W.	*An introduction to Development.* Curser Press, 1970
Fichter, J.H.	*Sociology.* Chicago: University of Chicago Press, 1937
Frank, A.G.	*Capitalism and Underdevelopment.* New York, Monthly Review Press, 1967
Goldschmidt, W. (ed.)	*The United States and Africa.* London & New York: Fredreick Praeger, Inc., 1963
Goldsthorpe, J. E.	*The Sociology of the Third World Disparity and Involvement.* Cambridge, CUP, 1975

Graiule, M.	*Conversation with Ogotemmeli*. London, OUP for IAI, 1951
Griffin, Keith	*Underdevelopment in Spanish America*. London, George Allen Unwin Press, 1969
Griffin, Keith	Underdevelopment in History in Charles K. Wilber (ed.) *The Political Economy of Development and Underdevelopment*. New York, 1973.
Guindi, F.E.	*Religion and Culture*. U.S.A, WMC Brown, 1977
Gutierrez, G.	*A Theology of Liberation*. London: S.C.M. Press, 1974
Ikoku, E.	*African Development with Human Face*. London, African Press, 1976
Jaguaribe, H.	*Economic and Political Development: A theoretical Approach and Brazilian Case Study*. Cambridge: Harvard University Press, 1968
Johnson, D.L.	*The Sociology of Change and Reaction in Latin America*. New York, 1973.
Kalu, O.U.	Tradition and Revolutionary Change. *Ikenga: Journal of African Studies*. Vol. 3, Nos. 1 & 2, 1975
Kay, G.	*Capitalism and Underdevelopment: A Marxist Analysis*. London: Macmillan Press, 1980
McKenzie, P.R.	*Inter-Religious Encounter in West Africa*. Leicester: Blackfriars Press, 1976
Mussen, P.H.	*The Psychological Development of the Child*. New Jersey, 1963
Nnoli, O.	*Path to Nigerian Development*. Darkar: Codesria, 1981
O'Brien, R.S.	*The Political Economy of Underdevelopment: Dependence in Senegal*. London, Sage Books, 1979.
Rhodes, R. (ed.)	*Imperialism and Underdevelopment: A Reader*. New York, Monthly Review Press, 1970.
Rodney, W.	*How Europe Underdeveloped Africa*. London, Bogle-L'Overture Publications. 1972
Rotbert, Rotberg	*Africa and Its Explorers: Motives, Methods and Impact*. Cambridge, Mass., 1970

Rothko, Chapel — Colloquium Towards a new Strategy for Development. New York: Pergaman Press, 1979

Scharf, Betty R. — The Sociological Study of Religion. London, Hutchinson University Library, 1976.

Selznick, Broom — The Principles of Sociology. New York, 1970

Torado, M.T. — *Economic Development in the Third World: An Introduction to the problems and policies in a global Perspective.* London, Longman, 1977

Taylor, E.B. — *Primitive Culture, Vol. 1.* London, 1871

Uchendu, V.C. — *Dependency and Underdevelopment in West Africa.* Leiden, E.J. Brill, 1980

Westermann, D. — *Africa and Christianity.* London, O.U.P. 1937

Wilson, M. — *Religion and Transformation of Society.* Cambridge, CUP, 1971

Zunini, G. — *Man and his Religion: Aspects of Religious Psychology.* London, 1969

B - European Contacts with Africa: Their views and African Nationalist Reactions.

Ajayi, J.F.A. — *Christian Missions in Nigeria 1841 –1891: The making of a new elite.* London, Longmans, 1965

Barbot, John — A description of the coasts of North and South Guinea 1732 in *A Collection of Voyages Travel, Vol. V.* London, Meppicurs Churchill, MDCC11. Printed for Henry Lintot and John Osborne, 1746.

Bovil, E.W. — *The Golden Trade of the Moors.* London, OUP, 1968

Blyden, E.W. — *Christianity, Islam and the Negro Race.* Edinburgh, University Press, 1887 -*African Life and Culture.* London. 1908

Burton, R.F. — *A Mission to Gelele, King of Dahome Vol.11.* London, Tinsley Brothers, 1864.

Butterfield, H. — *Christianity in European History.* London, 1951

Buxton, R.F. — *The African Slave Trade and Its Remedy.* London, 1840

Canot, Theodore — *Memories of a Slave Trader* (set down by Blantz Mayer and edited by A.W. Lawrence). London, George Newness Ltd Abridged edition, 1915

Claridge, W.W. — *A history of Gold Coast and Ashanti Vol. 1*. London, John Murray, 1975

Davidson, B. — *Black Mother.* London, Longmans 1961

Ellis, A.B. — *A history of the Gold Coast of West Africa.* London and Dublin, Curson Press Ltd. 1891. New Edition, 1971

Esedebe, P.E. — Wilmot Blyden1832 – 1912 as a Pan-African Theorist. *Sierra Leone Studies, New Series,* Vol. 25, (July 1969)

Frankel, M.Yu — Edward Blyden and the concept of African Personality. *African Affairs*, 72, no. 292, (July 1974)

Hakluyth — *Principal Navigation.* 1599 edition, vol. 2

Hamdum, S. & N. King — *Ibn Battuta in Black Africa.* London, Rex Collin, 1975

Hargreaves, J.D. — *Prelude to the Partition of West Africa.* London, Macmillan and Co. 1963. (ed.)*France and West Africa.* London, Macmillan & Co. 1969.

Harris, J.E. (ed.) *Africa and Africans a seen by Classical Writers.* Washington D.C., Howard University Press, 1977

Hayford, J.E. Casely — *Cold Coasts' Institutions,* 1903. Reprinted, London: Frank Cass & Co., 1970

Hodgkin, T. — *Nigerian Perspective.* London, O.U.P. 1975

Holden, E. — *Blyden of Liberia: An Account of the Life and Labours of E.W. Blyden as recounted in letter and print.* New York: Vantage Press, 1966

Hutchinson, T.J. — *Impressions of West Africa.* 1858. Reprinted, London 1970

Iweh, N.S.S. — *Christianity, Culture and Colonialism.* Port Harcourt: College of Education Press, 1985

Kingsley, Mary H. — *West African Studies.* London, 1899. Reprinted 2nd Edition, London, Frank Cass, 1964

Lynch, Hollis R.   *Black Statesman: Selected Public Writings of E.W. Blyden* London, Frank Cass, 1971

Mazrui, Ali   *The African Condition: The Reith Lectures* London, Heinemann, Reprint 1982

Mobley, Robert A.   *The Ghanaian Image of the Missionary.* Leiden, E.J. Brill, 1970

Nisbet, R.A.   *Social Change and History.* London, OUP, 1969

Oliver, Roland   *The Missionary Factor in East Africa.* London, Longmans, 1952

Oliver, R. & Anthony Atmore *Africa since 1800.* Cambridge, CUP, 1967

Oliver, R & J.D. Fage   *A Short History of Africa.* Middlesex, Penguin Books, 1962

Ogot, B.A. & J.A. Kierran (eds.)   *A Survey of East African History.* Nairobi, East African Publishing House, 1968.

Parry, J.H.   *Europe and Wider World 1415 – 1715.* London, Hutchinson University Library, 1949, Reissued 1960.

Roth, Hing King   *Great Benin: Its Customs, Art and Horrors.* Halifax England, F. Kings and Sons, 1902.

Ryder, A.F.C.   *Materials for the study of African History in Portuguese Archives.* London, University of London, Press, 1965

Shaw F. (Lady Lugard)   *A Tropical Dependency.* London, Nesbit & Co. 1906

Sithole, Ndabaningi   *African Nationalism*, 2nd Edition. London, OUP, 1983

Walter, R.   *The Holy Ghost Fathers*, Dublin: Rock College. 1933

West, Richard   *Back to Africa: A History of Sierra Leone and Liberia.* London: Jonathan Cape, 1970.

White, Charles   *Accounts of the Regular Graduations in Man.* London, 1799

C - AFRICAN TRADITIONAL RELIGION AND CULTURE

Abraham, W.E.   *The Mind of Africa.* Chicago: University of Chicago Press, 1962

Amadi, Elechi   *Ethics in Nigerian Society.* London, Heinemann, 1983

Awolalu, J.O.   *Yoruba Religion and Sacrificial Rites.* London, Longman, 1979

Beir, Ulli   *African Mud Sculpture.* London, 1963

Booth, N.S. Jr. (ed.)   *African Religions: A Symposium.* London, NOK 1981

Danquah, J.B.   *Akan Doctrine of God.* 2nd Edition, London, Frank Cass, 1968

Douglas, Mary (ed.)   *Witchcraft Confession and Accusations.* London, Tavistock Publications, 1970

Eliade, M.   *The Myth of Eternal Return.* Princeton: University Press, 1974

Evans-Prichard, E.E.   *Witchcraft, Oracles and Magic among the Azande.* Oxford, The Clarendon Press, 1937

——————   Nuer Religion. Oxford: O.U.P., 1956

Field, M.J.   *Religion and Medicine of the Ga People.* London: OUP, 1961

Gluckman,   Max *Custom and Conflict in Africa.* Oxford, Blackwell and Molt, 1960

Idowu, E.B.   *Olodumare: God in Yoruba Belief.* London, Longmans, 1962, *African Traditional Religion: A Definition.* London, SCM, 1973

Ilogu, E.C.O.   *Christianity and Igbo Culture.* London & NY, NOK Publishers, 1974

Ikenga-Metuh, E.   *God and Man in African Religion.* London: Geoffrey Chapman, 1981

Ikenga-Metuh,E.   *African Religions in Western Conceptual Scheme.* Ibadan, Pastoral Institute, 1985

——————— (ed.)   *Gods in Retreat: Models of Religious Change in Africa.* Enugu-Nigeria, Fourth Dimension Publishers, 1986.

Kalu, O.U.(ed.)   *African Cultural Development.* Enugu: Fourth
                         Dimension Publishers, 1978.
Kiev, Ari (ed)   *Magic, Faith and Healing.* New York: Free press,
                         1964
Leith-Ross, Sylvia   *African Women: A study of the Igbo of Nigeria.*
                         London Routledge and Kegan Paul, 1935,
                         Reprinted, 1981.
Mair, Lucy (ed.)   *African Societies.* Cambridge, CUP 1974
Maclean, Una   Magical Medicine: A Nigerian Case Study.
                         London: Penguin Books, 1971. Reprinted, 1985
Middleton, J& E.H.Winter (ed.)   *Witchcraft and Sacrifices in Africa.* London:
                         Oxford University Press, 1969
Mbiti, J.S.   *African Religions and Philosophy.* London,
                         Heinemann, 1969
_____   *Concepts of God in Africa.* London, SPCK 1970
_____   *New Testament Eschatology in an African Background.*
                         London, SPCK. 1971
Nadel, S.F.   *Nupe Religion.* London, Routledge and Kegan
                         Paul. 1954.
Parrinder, E.G.   *West African Religion.* London, Epworth Press.
                         1949
_____   *African Traditional Religion.* London, Sheldon Press.
                         1954.
_____   *Africa's Three Religions.* London, Sheldon Press.
                         1976
P'Bitek, Okot.   *African Religions in Western Scholarship.* Nairobi,
                         East African Publishing Bureau. 1970.
Ranger, T.O. & I.N. Kimambo (eds.)   *The Historical Study of African
                         Religion.* London Heinemann, 1972
Onunwa, U.R.   *Studies in Igbo Religion.* Obosi Nigeria, Pacific
                         Publishers, 1990.
Onunwa, U.R.   *African Spirituality: An Anthology of Igbo Religious
                         Myths.* Darmstadt Germany. Thesen Verlag
                         Wowincle, 1992
Onwuejeogwu, M.A.   *An Igbo Civilization: Nri Kingdom and Hegemony.*
                         London Ethnographica, 1981.

Rattray, R.S.   *Religion and Art in Ashanti.* London, 1937

Sarpong, P.   *Sacred Stools of the Akan.* Kumasi: Ghana
                         Publishing Corporations, 1971.

Sawyerr, H.   *God: Ancestor or Creator?* London, Longmans. 1970

Shaw, T.   *Igbo-Ukwu: An Account of Archaeological Discoveries in
                         Eastern Nigeria Vol. 1.* London: Faber and Faber,
                         1967.

_____   *Unearthing Igbo-Ukwu.* Ibadan, Oxford University
                         Press, 1967.

Shorter, Aylward   *African Christian Theology.* Gt. Britain, Geoffrey
                         Chapman, 1975.

Smith, E.W. (ed.)   *African Ideas of God.* London, Edinburgh House
                         Press, 1950. Reprinted, 1961, 1978.

Talbot, P.A.   *The Peoples of Southern Nigeria, Vol. 111. (Ethnology).*
                         London, OUP, 1926.

Taylor, J.V.   *The Primal Vision: Christian Presence and African
                         Religion.* ondon, SCM Press. 1963.

Temples, P.   *Bantu Philosophy.* Paris, Presence Africaine. 1959.

Uchendu, V.C.   *The Igbo of Southeastern Nigeria.* New York.
                         Rinehardt and Winston, 1965.

Zahan, Dominique.   *The Religion, Spirituality and Thought of Traditional
                         Africa.* London and Chicago. The University of
                         Chicago Press, 1970.